THE ECUMENICAL GRAIL PSALTER

The Benedictine Monks of Conception Abbey

GIA PUBLICATIONS, INC.

CHICAGO

The Ecumenical Grail Psalter

G-9089
ISBN: 978-1-62277-170-7

The Ecumenical Grail Psalter is *not approved for liturgical use
in the Catholic Church*, which retains for its liturgical use the
original *Revised Grail Psalms* as approved by both the USCCB
and Congregation for Divine Worship and the Discipline of
the Sacraments.

For reprint information, visit www.giamusic.com/egp

Printed in the United States of America.

INTRODUCTION TO
THE ECUMENICAL GRAIL PSALTER

The Songs of Israel—The Songs of the Church

In the late 1940s, Father Patrick Cummins, OSB, a monk of Conception Abbey and a scholar and translator of Scripture in his own right, wrote the following definition in the Introduction to his own unpublished translation of the Book of Psalms:

> What is a psalm? Is it a prayer? A rhythmic prayer? A hymn? An oriental hymn? A Semitic hymn? A Hebrew hymn? The answer to all these questions is an ascending Yes. Hence, if we look at human literature as an ascending pyramid, then that pyramid is crowned by the Psalter. [Human beings] are most godlike when [they] sing to God. And among those who sing to God the Hebrew psalmist stands highest. In universality of sentiment, in keenness of conception, in rhythm of speech, in beauty of imagery, the Hebrew singer has no rivals.

The Psalms have been the prayer book of both Jews and Christians from their beginnings as peoples of faith and worship. The Gospels make clear that Jesus himself used and prayed the Psalms during his earthly life, quoting from them more than from any other book of Scripture. The old adage *Lex orandi lex credendi*—which means "the way we pray is the way we believe"—suggests how significant these prayers have been in the formation of communities of believers. The Book of Psalms provides words that bring meaning to our search for God in all of life's circumstances: in fear or joy, struggle or hope, pain or praise, despair or thanksgiving. Though some of these texts have been used for more than two millennia, the prayers of the Psalter retain a freshness that enables them to speak with poignant clarity to each succeeding generation, drawing those who read them into the deepest purpose of human life: to abide in the presence of God.

How often in life do we find ourselves struggling to find words that express the manifold movements of the human heart! The Psalms provide access to that unique chamber of the heart where one stands most free and open before God. To our surprise, we find ourselves thinking, "These words express my inmost thoughts and feelings better than I could myself. They say what I want to say to God." The character of the Psalms is universal and classic, touching the human heart and giving voice to the most intimate motions of our souls before the One who is transcendent and immanent, incomprehensible yet alarmingly close. The Psalms take us from the heights of praise to the depths of distress with words that invariably foster a life-giving hope. They are inspired!

Rightly have the Psalms been called a school of prayer. These prayers give voice to many of the experiences presented in the stories of the Bible—they come to us as words that have already been cried, shouted, and sung throughout the centuries by people of faith. Human struggles with encompassing illness, imminent death, implacable enemies, and hostile powers find voice in the Psalms, which give expression to the fears and uncertainties that trouble the human condition. Similarly, the joy of victory, gratitude for prayers answered, and wonder at the marvels of creation all enter into the praise that is lifted up to God who brings life into being and rules the created world. The Psalms attest with unshakable conviction that the one and almighty God who touches every movement of history and each human life is the focus of all praise, the healer of all ills, and the source of all blessing.

The Psalms, then, are the prayer book of the Bible. They are appropriate responses to every situation encountered in the pages of sacred Scripture. In Christian congregations, having heard the word of God proclaimed in the readings, we respond with a psalm; its words echo those of the reading, lifting our hearts in prayer. As God has spoken to the assembly through the sacred word, so through the psalm do the people respond to God. Such dialogue is the heart of any relationship with God. The Psalms are an instrument of that dialogue when prayed by people of faith.

To the superlative status of the Psalms as literary expression, we may add the observation that the various genres or literary forms found in them express the wide-ranging life situations and the varying moods of the person of faith before God. The *hymn* lifts up praise to the God who has created the world and all its wonders. The *lament* brings before God the pain of alienation from God and neighbor, the struggle with doubts and fears, the anger that rises from disgrace and mistreatment, the fear of threatening illness and approaching death, the anguish of both individual loss and communal tribulation. The *thanksgiving* reminds the community that gratitude is owed to God who hears and answers those in need. The *wisdom* psalms reflect the insight and spiritual understanding that fosters a life of faith, hope, and love.

Many of the Psalms open with unfamiliar expressions like "A *mitzmor* of David, with instrumental music, on the *gittith*." The names of Korah (Psalms 42, 44–49) and Asaph (Psalm 50, 73–83), often attached to such expressions, identify two of the musical guilds of the Jerusalem temple, where the Psalms were originally prayed. Many of these phrases indicate that the Psalms were meant to be sung, often with specified musical accompaniment. The Hebrew title for the Book of Psalms is *Sepher Tehillim*, or "a Book of Sung Praises," further indicating how these prayers were expected to be rendered. Any text is clothed and elevated by music; melody holds a special power to express what may not be possible for spoken words alone. It gives added expression that not only enhances the meaning but also raises the words to the level of inspiring prayer. This truth provides yet another insight into the profound message of the Psalms. They were created to be sung, which gives the words a second soul.

As songs of the early Church, the Psalms were not merely prayer, however; they were prophecy as well. In Luke's account of the risen Christ appearing and speaking to his disciples in Jerusalem, Jesus affirms: "'These are my words that I spoke to you while I was still with you, that everything written about me in the law of Moses and in the prophets and psalms must be fulfilled.' Then he opened their minds to understand the scriptures" (Luke 24:44 NRSV). The authors of the New Testament use the Psalms extensively to speak of the mystery of Jesus Christ as Messiah, the Anointed One.[1] The Psalms hold a key to understanding Jesus as the long-awaited Messiah. And as the early Church began to develop its yearly round of celebrating the life, suffering, death, and resurrection of Christ, the *messianic* psalms played a substantial role in unfolding that great mystery of faith.

In Praise of the 1963 Grail Psalms

The Grail Psalms (1963) provided one of the most successful of the vernacular texts to emerge from the liturgical reforms of the 1960s. These texts had originally been translated into English from the Psalms of the French *Bible de Jérusalem*; they proved remarkably sensitive to the requirements of choral recitation and chant, were adaptable to the requirements of varied musical settings, and were expressed in a literary style that was easily accessible to ordinary readers. The 1963 Grail Psalms became a primary vehicle for Christian prayer; over the years since, they have come to shape the worship and spiritual life of countless communities and individuals in the English-speaking world. They opened the door by which many people could become familiar with the language and imagery of the Bible in ways that were inviting, enriching, and satisfying.

What are the qualities that distinguish the 1963 Grail Psalms? For many, the Grail Psalms became an avenue into understanding and appreciating the whole of the Old Testament. Hearing this account of how God was for the chosen people both victorious warrior and gentle shepherd,

---

[1] Several salient passages in which the New Testament authors quote the Psalms are: Mt 21:9// Mk11:9//Lk 19:38//Jn 12:13 quotes Ps 118:26; Mt 21:42//Mk 12:10–11//Lk 20:17 quotes Ps 118:22–23; Mt 22:44//Mk 12:36//Lk 20:42–43 quotes Ps 110:1; Mt 27:46 quotes Ps 22:2; Jn 19:24 quotes Ps 22:19; Jn 19:36 quotes Ps 34:19; Acts 2:34–35 quotes Ps 110:1; Acts 4:25–26 quotes Ps 2:1–2; Heb 1:5 quotes Ps 2:7; Heb 1:6 quotes Ps 97:7; Heb 1:7 quotes Ps 104:4 (LXX); Heb 1:8 quotes Ps 45:7–8; Heb 1:10–12 quotes Ps 102:26–28; Heb 1:13 quotes Ps 110:1; Heb 2:6–7 quotes Ps 8: 5–7.

the One who hears our single voice in prayer and who calls us to live faithfully—this made clear how intimate was the relationship each person shares with God. Simple expressions continue to resonate in the hearts of many who pray these texts, bespeaking their own prayer to God: "Be still and know that I am God" (Ps 46:11), "Create a pure heart in me, O God" (Ps 51:12), "Mercy and faithfulness have met, justice and peace have embraced" (Ps 85:11), "Friend and neighbor you have taken away; my one companion is darkness" (Ps 88:19), and "O LORD, you search me and you know me; you know my resting and my rising" (Ps 139:1–2a). Such phrases lend themselves to effortless recall, becoming the very fabric of the interior life.

The "sprung rhythm" in which the Grail Psalms were composed made them easy to recite in common (that is, in a group setting) and easy to sing as chant.[2] Setting aside the stricter expectations of more formal poetic conventions, this rhythmic style imitates regular speech patterns more closely. Sprung rhythm possesses in vocal use something both natural and beautiful, a quality of simplicity and regularity one finds in reading through the lines of a Grail Psalm. The very ebb and flow of the lines make these psalms conducive to prayer and reflection. And importantly, these rhythmic patterns bear a notable similarity to those in which the Hebrew psalms were composed and are still evident today when they are prayed aloud in the synagogue.

The language of the 1963 Grail Psalms was straightforward and accessible; the person in the pew did not need a background in scriptural theology to grasp the general import of the text. At the same time, its poetic quality and beauty also could inspire the sensitive reader to ponder on further levels these simple yet profound and noble expressions of faith. It gave those who prayed it a language steeped in the inspired word, language for petition, praise, thanksgiving, confidence, hope, courage, faith, sorrow,

---

[2] Sprung rhythm imitates natural speech patterns, designating a certain number of major accents per line, while having an unfixed number of unstressed syllables, with no more than four syllables between each foot. Gerard Manley Hopkins, the nineteenth-century British poet and Jesuit, coined the expression, calling it "the most natural of things" in spoken poetry.

human struggle before God, and love of God, neighbor, and creation. It gave people a form for their own internal conversation with God.

Why a Revision of the 1963 Grail Psalms?

The excellent qualities of the 1963 Grail Psalms might give rise to the question, Why make a revision? There are several compelling reasons. As with anything that has generated such positive appreciation, there are also negative criticisms to be made. While the rhythmic quality and consistency in the Grail Psalms merits praise, the sometimes strict adherence to these rhythmic patterns too frequently forced its translators to *paraphrase* the text rather than translate it literally. Our revision maintains the sprung rhythm while at the same time striving for a more authentic translation of many paraphrased lines. Those who have prayed the 1963 Grail Psalms for many years will find great similarities in this revision, but will also encounter some very different expressions of language in the newly translated elements.

Furthermore, considerable strides have been made in biblical scholarship since the 1950s and early 1960s, when the Grail translations were produced. We have come to a better understanding of many of the rhetorical devices used by the Hebrew psalmists, and these insights have been incorporated into the revision. Our understanding of the literary genres and patterns of thought found in the Psalms has also developed greatly; this too enables us to translate these ancient texts with greater accuracy.

And while building on the good and inspiring elements of the first edition has the potential to provide continuity for those who have prayed the Grail Psalms during these past five decades, we must be cognizant of those who will use this Psalter in the future. It is our genuine hope that this revision of the Grail Psalms will be an effective vehicle for prayer, contemplation, and interior renewal of heart. Even as it seeks to present more authentic renderings of the ancient texts, it also hopes to provide more inclusive forms of expression—forms that are often truer to the original Hebrew than were the 1963 Grail Psalms. If this revision of the 1963 Grail Psalms helps to forward the renewal that every heart constantly seeks, it will have fulfilled its purpose.

We have also created a "Singing Version" of *The Ecumenical Grail Psalter*. The edition indicates the accents of the sprung rhythm for recitation and chanting of the Psalms. It is our hope that these marked accents will facilitate a prayerful and inspiring chanting or reading of the Psalms for communities who pray the Liturgy of the Hours in common, or for individuals who might wish to recite or chant them aloud.

Why an Ecumenical Edition of *The Revised Grail Psalms*?

On 19 March 2010, the Congregation for Divine Worship and the Discipline of the Sacraments granted a *recognitio* (that is, permission for a text to be used in the Roman Catholic liturgy) to *The Revised Grail Psalms*. As noted above, this edition was prepared as a *liturgical translation*, intended for use in the Roman Catholic liturgy. Guiding principles for translation were provided by *Liturgiam Authenticam*, a document of the Congregation for Divine Worship and the Discipline of the Sacraments, and the process took into account the historical use of the Book of Psalms in the Church's liturgy. Thus while the translation is primarily based on the Hebrew text of the Psalms from the *Biblica Hebraica Stuttgartensia*, it is important to recognize that because of their influence on the Church's use of the Psalter, the texts of the Greek Septuagint and the Latin *Vulgata* and *Nova Vulgata* were also taken into account for this translation specifically intended for use in the Roman Catholic liturgy.

Within a year of its publication, Christian leaders from groups beyond the Roman Catholic communion expressed appreciation for certain aspects of the texts of *The Revised Grail Psalms*, particularly the poetic quality of the text and the sprung rhythm, which facilitates recitation, chant, and musical settings of the texts. Among these leaders were an Episcopalian bishop, a bishop of the Evangelical Lutheran Church of America, the president of a Baptist seminary, and the academic dean of a Calvinist seminary. They further inquired if we might consider publishing another edition of *The Revised Grail Psalms*, focusing more directly on the original Hebrew while seeking a more inclusive final text of the sort preferred in the current worship of their respective communions.

We consulted with the undersecretary of the Congregation for Divine Worship and the Discipline of the Sacraments, who indicated that he considered the project a worthwhile endeavor, suggesting that it first be vetted by the US Conference of Catholic Bishops through their offices of Divine Worship and Ecumenical and Interreligious Affairs. These offices responded in the affirmative, stipulating that, while recognizing the value of the project as an ecumenical endeavor, it would be necessary to state clearly that *The Ecumenical Grail Psalter* is *not approved for liturgical use in the Catholic Church*, which retains for its liturgical use the original *Revised Grail Psalms* as approved by both the USCCB and the Congregation for Divine Worship and the Discipline of the Sacraments. Thus *The Ecumenical Grail Psalter* came to be.

At this point it must be admitted that an ecumenical edition of *The Revised Grail Psalms*, which strives for a nonexclusive text that avoids unnecessary gender-specific references to the Deity or to the human person in general terms, is necessarily going to have to admit some paraphrasis in its own rendering of the text into English. We have sought to strike a balance here, avoiding masculine terminology when referring to God wherever possible, and allowing gender-specific terms only when they refer directly to historical persons who are males. This includes those prophetic texts that have come to be associated with Jesus Christ in the tradition of interpretation. On the other had, it was our editorial decision to retain the literary use of the feminine pronoun when referring to Jerusalem (or other cities or comparable political entities; cf. Ps 46:6; 48:4,13–14; 68:32; 87:5; 102:15; 125:2; 132:15–16), to retain the association with historic and biblical custom of referring to such entities in the feminine, particularly as "daughter," as in "daughter Zion" and other such designations (cf. Ps 9:15; 73:28; also 45:13; 137:8).

A Word for Those Unfamiliar with the Book of Psalms

Every day, people are reading or hearing the Psalms for the first time. Some have told me that their first encounter from the Book of Psalms as a child or adolescent left them feeling that they did not understand it, and they never felt drawn back to it. Others are aware of the Psalms but simply have not read or prayed seriously with them. Yet interest in this biblical book of prayers continues to grow, and with good reason.

One effective way to appropriate the prayers and images of the Psalter is to use them to express one's own human need for God. So often we find ourselves in circumstances that compel us to communicate our situation to the Lord. As we slowly come to realize that all blessing is from God, we discover within ourselves the need to lift up words of praise and thanks to our Maker and Lord. In moments of sadness, disappointment, frustration, and even anger, almighty God is the one to whom we turn, hoping for a reversal of our troubled situation. In the Psalter are many such expressions of human need before God; making such prayers our own is the only way to become truly familiar with these prayers that people of faith have used for centuries both in moments of private appeal and in joyous community celebrations.

Below is a short list of different circumstances that frequently lead one to prayer. For each of these, we have suggested corresponding Psalms to give appropriate expression to these circumstances. It is our hope that this might open new avenues of satisfying and enriching prayer for newcomer to the Psalms. The list is not definitive, but meant rather to present some of the best-known and most frequently used Psalms under familiar headings; you will see that some Psalms are listed more than once.

1. A Morning Prayer—Psalms 3, 5, 63, 143
2. An Evening Prayer—Psalms 130, 141
3. A Night Prayer—Psalms 4, 91, 134
4. Praise of God—Psalms 8, 66, 104, 135, 136, 145, 148, 150
5. Thanksgiving to God—Psalms 30, 34, 92, 111, 116, 118, 138
6. Prayer for Upright Living—Psalms 1, 15, 24, 37, 112

The Church has always intended that the community's use of the Psalms in congregational prayer serve as a source of inspiration for personal prayer as well. Integral to the reflective appropriation of the Scriptures is to pray directly from the biblical text. When the congregation prays a psalm together, it serves as the voice of the whole community responding to the voice of God that they have heard in the other biblical readings. We can certainly make use of the same method when we pray the Psalms privately: reading the text of the psalm, reflecting on it, and then lifting up to God our own words that arise from our meditative encounter with the text.

Reading and praying in this manner, placing the texts of the Psalms at the heart of our prayer, we are formed in the spirit of the Bible's own prayer book. Whether in community prayer or in prayer of the heart alone in one's room, these ancient prayers of synagogue and church have taught generations of faith-filled people the way of redemption as it is lived out in everyday life. Their universal message continues to inspire people to open wide their hearts to a God whose word to us is "ever ancient, ever new," as Saint Augustine so aptly put it. The Psalms become our daily companion in prayer and our daily conversation with the living God, who has created us for just that purpose.

Acknowledgments

When this work of the revision of the 1963 Grail Psalms was undertaken in 1998, we had no idea how extensive an effort would be required to bring it to a successful conclusion. The work of the monks of Conception Abbey involved in producing the work beyond translation included proofreading, musical considerations, and computer layout, as well as suggestions to improve felicity of expression in both grammar and syntax of both the text and ancillary documents. And finally, it is worth noting that the monks of Conception Abbey prayed the texts of *The Revised Grail Psalms* for several years before the text was finalized, engaging them with heart and soul, and offering suggestions for improvement and words of encouragement for what we hoped would eventually emerge as yet one more contribution from the Benedictine Order to the ongoing growth and development of the Church's liturgy.

The three most recent popes have indicated their conviction that Benedictine monks are especially situated to engage in the important work of ecumenical and interreligious dialogue and prayer. The monks of Conception Abbey are honored to have been invited to participate in an endeavor that supports the ongoing ecumenical work of so many Christian communities, especially as it involves our shared prayer and the worship of the one God.

We offer our sincere thanks to all those who read through this translation and offered their suggestions and reactions. Various Christian communities were consulted in this endeavor in the hope that this translation would meet their needs, hopes, and expectations for an ecumenical psalter. We continue to hope that such will be the case. May God be praised in all ways and at all times.

Abbot Gregory J. Polan, OSB
Conception Abbey

BOOK ONE
OF THE PSALTER

Psalm 1

¹ Blessed indeed are those
   who follow not the counsel of the wicked,
   nor stand in the path with sinners,
   nor abide in the company of scorners,
² but whose delight is the law of the LORD,
   and who ponder God's law day and night.

³ Such people are like trees that are planted
   beside the flowing waters,
   that yield their fruit in due season,
   and whose leaves shall never fade;
   and all that they do shall prosper.

⁴ Not so are the wicked, not so!
   For they, like winnowed chaff,
   shall be driven away by the wind.

⁵ When the wicked are judged they shall not rise,
   nor shall sinners in the council of the righteous;
⁶ for the LORD knows the way of the righteous,
   but the way of the wicked will perish.

Psalm 2

1 Why do the nations conspire,
   and the peoples plot in vain?
2 They arise, the rulers of the earth;
   nobles plot against the Lᴏʀᴅ and his Anointed.
3 "Let us burst asunder their fetters.
   Let us cast off from us their chains."

4 The One who sits in the heavens laughs;
   the Lᴏʀᴅ derides and mocks them.
5 Then the Lord will speak in his anger,
   and strike them with terror and rage.
6 "It is I who have appointed my king
   on Zion, my holy mountain."

7 I will announce the decree of the Lᴏʀᴅ:
   The Lᴏʀᴅ said to me, "You are my Son.
   It is I who have begotten you this day."

[8] "Ask of me and I will make nations your heritage,
   and the ends of the earth as your possession.
[9] With a rod of iron you will rule them;
   like a potter's jar you will shatter them."

[10] So now, O rulers, understand;
   take warning, nobles of the earth.
[11] Serve the LORD with fear;
   exult with trembling, pay your homage,
[12] lest God be angry and you perish on the way
   in the sudden blaze of God's anger.

Blessed are all who trust in God!

Psalm 3

1 *A Psalm of David as he is fleeing from his son Absalom.*

2 How many are my foes, O Lord!
   How many are rising up against me!
3 How many are saying about me,
   "There is no salvation for you in God."

4 But you, Lord, are a shield about me,
   my glory, who lift up my head.
5 I cry aloud to the Lord,
   from whose holy mountain comes my answer.

6 I lie down, I sleep and I wake,
   for the Lord upholds me.
7 I will not fear even thousands of people
   who are ranged on every side against me.

   Arise, Lord; save me, my God,
8 you who strike all my foes on the cheek,
   you who break the teeth of the wicked!
9 Salvation belongs to the Lord;
   may your blessing be on your people!

Psalm 4

¹ *For the Choirmaster. With stringed instruments.
A Psalm of David.*

² O God of my righteousness, give answer when I
    call;
  from anguish you released me, have mercy, hear my
    prayer!

³ O you people, how long will my glory be
    dishonored,
  will you love what is futile and seek what is false?

⁴ Know that the LORD works wonders for the faithful;
  the LORD will hear me whenever I call out.

⁵ Tremble, do not sin: ponder on your bed and be
    still.
⁶ Offer a righteous sacrifice, and trust in the LORD.

⁷ "O that we might see better times" many say.
  Lift up the light of your face on us, O LORD.

⁸ You have put into my heart a greater joy
  than abundance of grain and new wine can provide.

⁹ In peace I will lie down and fall asleep,
  for you alone, O LORD, make me dwell in safety.

Psalm 5

¹ *For the Choirmaster. With flutes. A Psalm of David.*

² To my words give ear, O Lord;
   give heed to my sighs.
³ Attend to the sound of my cry,
   my Sovereign and my God.

⁴ To you do I pray, O Lord.
   In the morning you hear my voice;
   in the morning I plead and watch before you.

⁵ You are no God who delights in evil;
   no sinner is your guest.
⁶ The boastful shall not stand before your eyes.

⁷ All who do evil you despise;
   all who lie you destroy.
   Whoever speaks lies and sheds blood
   the Lord detests.

⁸ Yet through the greatness of your faithful love,
   I enter your house. ˙
   I bow down before your holy temple,
   in awe of you.

⁹ Lead me, LORD, in your righteousness,
  because of my foes;
  make straight your way before me.

¹⁰ No truth can be found in their mouths,
  their heart is all malice,
  their throat a wide-open grave;
  with their tongue they flatter.

¹¹ Declare them guilty, O God.
  Let them fail in their designs.
  Drive them out for their many transgressions,
  for against you have they rebelled.

¹² All who take refuge in you shall be glad,
  and ever cry out their joy.
  You shelter them; in you they rejoice,
  those who love your name.
¹³ It is you who bless the righteous, O LORD,
  you surround them with your favor like a shield.

Psalm 6

¹ *For the Choirmaster. With stringed instruments,*
  upon the Eighth Chord. A Psalm of David.

² O Lᴏʀᴅ, do not rebuke me in your anger;
  reprove me not in your rage.
³ Have mercy on me, Lᴏʀᴅ, for I languish.
  Lᴏʀᴅ, heal me; my bones are shaking,
⁴ and my soul is greatly shaken.

  But you, O Lᴏʀᴅ, how long?
⁵ Return, Lᴏʀᴅ, rescue my soul.
  Save me in your gracious love.
⁶ For in death there is no remembrance of you;
  who can give you praise from Sheol?

⁷ I am exhausted with my groaning;
  every night I drench my bed with tears,
  I bedew my couch with weeping.
⁸ My eyes waste away with grief;
  they have grown weak surrounded by all my foes.

⁹ Leave me, all who do evil,
  for the Lᴏʀᴅ heeds the sound of my weeping.
¹⁰ The Lᴏʀᴅ has heard my plea;
  The Lᴏʀᴅ will receive my prayer.
¹¹ All my foes will be shamed and greatly shaken,
  suddenly put to shame.

Psalm 7

1 *A Lament of David that he chanted to the LORD on*
    account of Cush, the Benjaminite.

2 O LORD, my God, I take refuge in you.
    Save and rescue me from all my pursuers,
3 lest like a lion they tear me apart,
    and drag me off with no one to rescue me.

4 If I have done this, O LORD, my God,
    if there is wrong on my hands,
5 if I have paid back evil for good,
    or plundered my foe without cause:

6 Then let my foes pursue my soul and seize me,
    let them trample my life to the ground,
    and lay my honor in the dust.

7 O LORD, rise up in your anger;
    be exalted in your fury toward my foes.
    Awake for me the justice you have ordered.
8 Let the company of peoples gather round you,
    as you take your seat above them on high.

9 The LORD is judge of the peoples.
    Give judgment for me, O LORD,
    for I am righteous and blameless of heart.

10 Put an end to the evil of the wicked!
   Make the righteous stand firm.
   It is you who test mind and heart,
   O righteous God!

11 God is a shield before me,
   who saves the upright of heart.
12 God is a judge, just and powerful and patient,
   not exercising anger every day.

13 Against someone who does not repent,
   God will sharpen a sword,
   bend a bow and make ready.
14 For such a one God prepares deadly weapons,
   barbing arrows with fire.

15 Here are the ones who conceive iniquity,
   pregnant with malice, giving birth to lies.
16 They dig a pit and bore it deep,
   and in the trap they have made they fall.
17 For their malice recoils on their own heads;
   on their own skulls their violence falls.

18 I thank the LORD for divine righteousness,
   and sing to the name of the LORD, the Most
       High.

Psalm 8

1 *For the Choirmaster. Upon the* gittith. *A Psalm of David.*

2 O LORD, our Sovereign, how majestic
   is your name through all the earth!

   Your majesty is set above the heavens.
3 From the mouths of children and of babes
   you fashioned praise to foil your enemy,
   to silence the foe and the rebel.

4 When I see the heavens, the work of your fingers,
   the moon and the stars which you arranged,
5 what are human beings that you keep them in mind,
   mortal creatures that you care for them?

6 Yet you have made them little lower than the angels;
   with glory and honor you crowned them,
7 gave them power over the works of your hands:
   you put all things under their feet,

8 All of them, sheep and oxen,
   yes, even the cattle of the fields,
9 birds of the air, and fish of the sea
   that make their way through the seas.

10 O LORD, our Sovereign, how majestic
    is your name through all the earth!

Psalm 9

¹ *For the Choirmaster. In the manner of a Chant*
   Mut Labben. *A Psalm of David.*

² I will praise you, LORD, with all my heart;
   all your wonders I will recount.
³ I will rejoice in you and be glad,
   and sing psalms to your name, O Most High.

⁴ See how my enemies turn back,
   how they stumble and perish before you.
⁵ You upheld the justice of my cause;
   you sat enthroned, judging with righteousness.

⁶ You have rebuked the nations, destroyed the wicked;
   you have wiped out their name forever and ever.
⁷ The foe is destroyed, eternally ruined.
   You uprooted their cities; their memory has
      perished.

⁸ But the LORD sits enthroned forever,
   and has set up a throne for judgment.
⁹ God will judge the world with righteousness,
   and will govern the peoples with equity.

¹⁰ For the oppressed, the LORD will be a stronghold,
   a stronghold in times of distress.
¹¹ Those who know your name will trust you;
   you will not forsake those who seek you, O LORD.

¹² Sing psalms to the LORD who dwells in Zion,
　　whose mighty works are revealed among the
　　　　peoples,
¹³ for the Avenger of Blood has remembered them,
　　has not forgotten the cry of the poor.

¹⁴ Have mercy on me, O LORD;
　　see how I suffer from my foes,
　　you who raise me from the gates of death,
¹⁵ that I may recount all your praise
　　at the gates of daughter Zion,
　　and rejoice in your salvation.

¹⁶ The nations have fallen in the pit which they
　　　　made;
　　their feet have been caught in the snare they laid.
¹⁷ The LORD is known for the judgment enacted.
　　The wicked are snared by the work of their
　　　　hands.

¹⁸ Let the wicked go down to Sheol,
　　all the nations forgetful of God:
¹⁹ for the needy shall not always be forgotten,
　　nor the hopes of the poor ever perish.

²⁰ Arise, O LORD, let human strength not prevail!
　　Let the nations be judged before you.
²¹ Strike them with terror, O LORD;
　　let the nations know they are only human.

Psalm 10 *(9:22–39)*

¹ Why, O Lord, do you stand far off,
  and hide yourself in times of distress?
² The poor are devoured by the pride of the wicked;
  they are caught in the schemes that others have
    made.

³ For the wicked boast of their souls' desires;
  the covetous blaspheme and spurn the Lord.
⁴ The wicked say with pride, "God will not punish.
  There is no God." Such are their thoughts.

⁵ Their path is ever untroubled;
  your judgments are on high, far removed.
  All those who oppose them, they deride.
⁶ In their hearts they think, "Never shall we falter;
  never shall misfortune be our lot."

⁷ Their mouths are full of cursing, guile, oppression;
  under their tongues are deceit and evil.
⁸ They sit in ambush in the villages;
  in hidden places, they murder the innocent.

  The eyes of the wicked keep watch for the
    helpless.
⁹ They lurk in hiding like lions in their lairs;
  they lurk in hiding to seize the poor,
    they seize the poor and draw them to their net.

¹⁰ They crouch, preparing to spring,
and the helpless fall prey to their strength.
¹¹ They say in their hearts, "God forgets,
turns away from us, and never sees a thing."

¹² Arise, O Lord; lift up your hand, O God!
Do not forget the poor!
¹³ Why should the wicked spurn God,
and say in their hearts, "You will not call us to
account"?

¹⁴ But you have seen the trouble and sorrow.
You note it; you take it in your hands.
The helpless one relies on you,
for you are the helper of the orphan.

¹⁵ Break the arm of the wicked and the sinner!
Pursue their wickedness till nothing remains!
¹⁶ The Lord is Sovereign forever and ever.
Nations shall perish from the land of the Lord.

¹⁷ O Lord, you have heard the desire of the poor.
You strengthen their hearts; you turn your ear
¹⁸ to give right judgment for the orphan and
oppressed,
so that no one on earth may strike terror again.

Psalm 11 (10)

¹ *For the Choirmaster. Of David.*

In the LORD I have taken refuge.
How can you say to my soul,
"Fly like a bird to the mountain!

² "Look, the wicked are bending their bow!
They are fixing their arrow on the string,
to shoot the upright of heart in the dark.
³ Foundations once destroyed,
what can the righteous do?"

⁴ The LORD is in his holy temple;
in heaven is the throne of the LORD,
whose eyes behold the world,
whose gaze inspects the human race.

⁵ The LORD inspects the righteous and the wicked,
and hates the lover of violence,
⁶ sending fire and brimstone on the wicked,
a scorching wind to fill their cup.
⁷ For the LORD is righteous and loves righteous
deeds;
the upright shall behold the face of God.

Psalm 12 (11)

¹ *For the Choirmaster. Upon the Eighth Chord.*
A Psalm of David.

² Save me, O LORD, for the holy ones are no more;
the faithful have vanished from the human race.
³ They babble vanities, one to another,
with cunning lips, with divided heart.

⁴ May the LORD destroy all cunning lips,
the tongue that utters boastful words,
⁵ Those who say, "We prevail with our tongue;
our lips are our own, who can command us?"

⁶ "For the poor who are oppressed and the needy
who sigh,
now will I arise," says the LORD;
"I will grant them the salvation for which they
long."
⁷ The words of the LORD are words without alloy,
silver from the furnace, seven times refined.

⁸ It is you, O LORD, who will keep us safe,
and protect us forever from this generation.
⁹ The wicked prowl on every side,
while baseness is exalted by the human race.

Psalm 13 *(12)*

¹ *For the Choirmaster. A Psalm of David.*

² How long, O LORD? Will you forget me forever?
   How long will you hide your face from me?
³ How long must I bear grief in my soul,
   have sorrow in my heart all day long?
   How long shall my enemy prevail over me?

⁴ Look, answer me, O LORD my God!
   Give light to my eyes lest I fall asleep in death;
⁵ lest my enemy say, "I have prevailed over you;"
   lest my foes rejoice when they see me fall.

⁶ As for me, I trust in your faithful love.
   Let my heart rejoice in your salvation.
⁷ I will sing to the LORD who has been bountiful
      with me.

Psalm 14 *(13)*

¹ *For the Choirmaster. A Psalm of David.*

The foolish have said in their hearts,
"There is no God."
Their deeds are corrupt, depraved;
no one does any good.

2 The LORD looks down from heaven
  on the human race,
  to see if any are wise,
  if any seek God.

3 All have gone astray,
  depraved, every one;
  there is no one who does any good;
  no, not even one.

4 Do none of the evildoers understand?
  They eat up my people as if eating bread;
  they never call out to the LORD.

5 There they shall tremble with fear,
  for God is with the righteous generation.
6 You may mock the plans of the poor,
  but their refuge is the LORD.

7 Oh, that the rescue of Israel might come from
    Zion.
  When the LORD brings about the people's return,
  then Jacob will be glad and Israel rejoice.

Psalm 15 *(14)*

¹ *A Psalm of David.*

Lord, who may abide in your tent,
and dwell on your holy mountain?

² Whoever walks without fault;
who does what is righteous,
and speaks with heartfelt truth.

³ Whoever does not slander with the tongue;
who does no wrong to a neighbor,
who casts no slur on a friend,
⁴ who looks with scorn on the wicked,
but honors those who fear the Lord.

Whoever keeps an oath, whatever the cost,
⁵ who lends no money at interest,
and accepts no bribes against the innocent.

Such a one shall never be shaken.

Psalm 16 *(15)*

¹ *A Miktam. Of David.*

Preserve me, O God, for in you I take refuge.
² I say to the Lord, "You are my Lord.
You are my good, you alone."

³ As for the holy ones who dwell in the land,
   they are noble, and in them I delight.
⁴ Those who choose other gods increase their
      sorrows.
   I will not take part in their offerings of blood.
   Nor will I take their names upon my lips.

⁵ O Lᴏʀᴅ, it is you who are my portion and cup;
   it is you yourself who secure my destiny.
⁶ Pleasant places are marked out for me:
   a fair heritage indeed is my lot!

⁷ I will bless the Lᴏʀᴅ who gives me counsel,
   who even at night directs my heart.
⁸ I keep the Lᴏʀᴅ before me always;
   with God at my right hand, I shall not be moved.

⁹ And so my heart rejoices, my soul is glad;
   even my body shall rest in safety.
¹⁰ For you will not abandon my soul to Sheol,
   nor let your holy one see corruption.

¹¹ You will show me the path of life,
   the fullness of joy in your presence,
   at your right hand, bliss forever.

Psalm 17 (16)

¹ *A Prayer of David.*

O LORD, hear a cause that is just,
pay heed to my cry.
Turn your ear to my prayer:
no deceit is on my lips.
² From you may my justice come forth.
Your eyes discern what is upright.

³ Search my heart and visit me by night.
Test me by fire, and you will find no wrong in me.

⁴ My mouth does not transgress as others do;
on account of the words of your lips,
I have avoided the paths of the violent.

⁵ I kept my steps firmly in your paths.
My feet have never faltered.

⁶ To you I call; for you will surely heed me, O God.
Turn your ear to me; hear my words.
⁷ Display your faithful love,
you who deliver from their foes
those who trust in your right hand.

⁸ Guard me as the apple of your eye.
   Hide me in the shadow of your wings
⁹ from the violent attack of the wicked.

   My foes encircle me with deadly intent.
¹⁰ Their hearts tight shut, their mouths speak
         proudly.
¹¹ They advance against me, and now they surround
      me.
   Their eyes watch to strike me to the ground.
¹² They are like a lion ready to claw,
   like some young lion crouched in hiding.

¹³ Arise, O LORD, confront them, strike them down!
   Let your sword deliver my soul from the wicked!
¹⁴ Let your hand, O LORD, deliver me
   from those whose portion in life is of this world.

   May what you have stored up for them fill their
         bellies;
   may their offspring be sated with its plenty,
   and let them leave what is left for their young.
¹⁵ As for me, I shall behold your face in
         righteousness;
   when I awake I shall be filled with the vision of
         your presence.

Psalm 18 (17)

¹ *For the Choirmaster. Of David, the servant of the*
    *L*ORD*, who spoke the words of this canticle to the*
    *L*ORD *when he had been freed from the power of*
    all his enemies and from the hand of Saul.
² *He said:*

I love you, LORD, my strength;
³ O LORD, my rock, my fortress, my savior;
  my God, my rock where I take refuge;
  my shield, my saving strength, my stronghold.
⁴ I cry out, "O praised be the LORD!"
  and see, I am saved from my foes.

⁵ The waves of death rose about me;
  the torrents of destruction assailed me;
⁶ the snares of Sheol surrounded me;
  the traps of death confronted me.

⁷ In my anguish I called to the LORD;
  I cried to my God for help.
  In the heavenly temple my voice was heard;
  my crying reached God's ears.

⁸ The earth then reeled and rocked;
  the mountains were shaken to their base,
  quaking at the anger of God,

⁹ from whose nostrils came forth smoke,
   from whose mouth came scorching fire;
   from this live coals were kindled.

¹⁰ God bent the heavens and came down,
   a cloud of thick darkness beneath,
¹¹ riding on a cherub in flight;
   soaring on the wings of the wind.

¹² The darkness served as a covering,
   the dark waters of the clouds as a tent.
¹³ A brightness shone out before the Lord,
   with hailstones and flashes of fire.

¹⁴ The LORD then thundered in the heavens;
   amid hail and coals of fire
   the voice of the Most High rang forth.
¹⁵ Shooting arrows, scattering the foe,
   flashing lightnings, God put them to flight.

¹⁶ The bed of the ocean was revealed;
   the foundations of the world were laid bare
   at your rebuke, O LORD,
   at the blast of the breath of your nostrils.

¹⁷ From on high God reached down and seized me,
   drew me forth from the mighty waters,
¹⁸ and saved me from my powerful foe,
   from my enemies, whose strength I could not match.

¹⁹ They assailed me in the day of my misfortune,
   but the LORD was my strong support,
²⁰ bringing me out to a place of freedom,
   saving me, indeed, with delight.

²¹ The LORD rewarded me because I was righteous,
   repaid me, for my hands were clean,
²² for I have kept the ways of the LORD,
   and have not fallen away from my God.

²³ For before me are all the judgments of God,
   whose commands I have not cast aside.
²⁴ I have been blameless before the Almighty;
   I have kept myself from guilt.
²⁵ You repaid me, O LORD, for I was righteous,
   and my hands were clean in your sight.

²⁶ With the faithful you show yourself faithful;
   with the blameless you show yourself blameless.
²⁷ With the sincere you show yourself sincere,
   but the cunning you outdo in shrewdness;
²⁸ for you save a lowly people,
   but bring low the eyes that are proud.

²⁹ It is you who give light to my lamp;
   the LORD my God lightens my darkness.
³⁰ With you I can crush the foe,
   with my God I can scale a wall.

31 The way of God is blameless;
   the word of the LORD is pure;
   God is a shield for all who trust.

32 For who is God but the LORD?
   Who is a rock but our God?
33 It is God who girds me with strength,
   and keeps my path free of blame,
34 Made my feet as swift as the deer's,
   able to stand firm on the heights.

35 God has trained my hands for battle,
   and my arms to bend the bronze bow.
36 You gave me your saving shield;
   with your right hand, you gave me support;
   you bent down to make me great.
37 You lengthened my steps beneath me;
   and my feet have never slipped.

38 I pursued and overtook my foes,
   never turning back till they were slain.
39 I struck them so they could not rise;
   they fell beneath my feet.

40 You girded me with strength for battle;
   you made my enemies fall beneath me.
41 You made my foes take flight;
   those who hated me I destroyed.

⁴² They cried out, but there was no one to save
      them,
   cried to the LORD, who did not answer.
⁴³ I crushed them fine as dust before the wind,
   trod them down like dirt in the streets.

⁴⁴ From the feuds of the people you delivered me,
   and put me at the head of the nations.
   People unknown to me served me;
⁴⁵ when they heard of me, they obeyed me.

   Foreign nations came to me cringing;
⁴⁶ foreign nations faded away.
   Trembling, they came forth from their
      strongholds.

⁴⁷ The LORD lives, and blest be my Rock!
   May the God of my salvation be exalted,
⁴⁸ the God who gives me redress
   and subdues the peoples under me.

⁴⁹ You saved me from my furious foes;
   you set me above my assailants;
   you saved me from the violent one.
⁵⁰ So I will praise you, LORD, among the nations;
   to your name will I sing a psalm.

⁵¹ The LORD gives great victories to the king,
   and shows gracious love for the anointed one,
   for David and his progeny forever.

Psalm 19 *(18)*

¹ For the Choirmaster. A Psalm of David.

² The heavens declare the glory of God,
  whose handiwork the firmament proclaims.
³ Day unto day conveys the message,
  and night unto night imparts the knowledge.

⁴ No speech, no word, whose voice goes unheeded;
⁵ their sound goes forth through all the earth,
  their message to the utmost bounds of the world.

⁶ There God has placed a tent for the sun;
  it comes forth like a bridegroom coming from his
    tent,
  rejoices like a champion to run its course.

⁷ At one end of the heavens is the rising of the sun;
  to its furthest end it runs its course.
  There is nothing concealed from its burning heat.

*　　*　　*

⁸ The law of the LORD is perfect;
  it revives the soul.
  The decrees of the LORD are steadfast;
  they give wisdom to the simple.

9 The precepts of the LORD are right;
   they gladden the heart.
   The command of the LORD is clear;
   it gives light to the eyes.

10 The fear of the LORD is pure,
   abiding forever.
   The judgments of the LORD are true;
   they are, all of them, righteous.

11 They are more to be desired than gold,
   than quantities of gold.
   And sweeter are they than honey,
   than honey flowing from the comb.

12 So in them your servant finds instruction;
   great reward is in their keeping.
13 But who can detect their own errors?
   From hidden faults acquit me.

14 From presumption restrain your servant;
   may it not rule me.
   Then shall I be blameless,
   clean from grave sin.

15 May the spoken words of my mouth,
   the thoughts of my heart,
   win favor in your sight, O LORD,
   my rock and my redeemer!

Psalm 20 (19)

² May the LORD answer you in time of trial;
   may the name of Jacob's God protect you,
³ sending you help from the holy place,
   and giving you support from Zion.

⁴ May God remember all your offerings,
   receive your sacrifice with favor,
⁵ give you your heart's desire,
   and fulfill every one of your plans.

⁶ May we ring out our joy at your victory,
   and raise banners in the name of our God.
   May the LORD grant all your prayers.

⁷ Now I know the anointed one is saved by the
      LORD,
   who answers from the holy heavens
   with the right hand of victory and might.

⁸ Some put their trust in chariots or horses,
   but we in the name of the LORD, our God.
⁹ They will collapse and fall,
   but we shall rise up and hold firm.
¹⁰ Grant salvation to the king, O LORD,
   give answer on the day we call.

Psalm 21 (20)

¹ *For the Choirmaster. A Psalm of David.*

² In your strength, O LORD, the king rejoices;
  how greatly your salvation makes him glad!
³ You have granted his heart's desire;
  you have not withheld the prayer of his lips.

⁴ You came to meet him with blessings of
    prosperity;
  you have set on his head a crown of pure gold.
⁵ He asked you for life and this you have given:
  days that will last from age to age.

⁶ In your salvation how great is his glory;
  you have bestowed upon him majesty and
    splendor;
⁷ you have granted him blessings forever,
  made him rejoice with the joy of your face.

⁸ The king has placed his trust in the LORD,
  through the love of the Most High is unshaken.

⁹ Your hand will find out all your foes,
   your right hand will find out those who hate you.
¹⁰ You will burn them like a blazing furnace
   on the day when you appear,
   and the LORD will consume them in anger:
   fire will swallow them up.

¹¹ You will wipe out their descendants from the
         earth,
   and their offspring from the human race.
¹² Though they planned evil against you,
   though they plotted, they shall not prevail.

¹³ For you will force them to retreat;
   at them you will aim with your bow.
¹⁴ O LORD, arise in your strength;
   we shall sing and praise your power.

Psalm 22 (21)

¹ *For the Choirmaster. In the manner of "The Doe at Daybreak." A Psalm of David.*

² My God, my God, why have you forsaken me?
 Why are you far from saving me,
 so far from my words of anguish?
³ O my God, I call by day and you do not answer;
 I call by night and I find no relief.

⁴ Yet you, O God, are holy,
 enthroned on the praises of Israel.
⁵ In you our ancestors put their trust;
 they trusted and you set them free.
⁶ When they cried to you, they escaped;
 in you they trusted and were not put to shame.

⁷ But I am a worm, not even human,
 scorned by everyone, despised by the people.
⁸ All who see me deride me;
 they curl their lips, they shake their heads:
⁹ "You trusted in the LORD, may you now be saved,
 yes, released, for in you God delights."

¹⁰ Yes, it was you who took me from the womb,
 kept me safe on my mother's breast.
¹¹ To you I was committed from birth;
 from my mother's womb, you have been my God.
¹² Stay not far from me;
 trouble is near, and there is no one to help.

¹³ Many bulls have surrounded me,
　　fierce bulls of Bashan close me in.
¹⁴ Against me they open wide their mouths,
　　like a lion, rending and roaring.

¹⁵ Like water I am poured out,
　　disjointed are all my bones.
　　My heart has become like wax,
　　it is melted within my breast.

¹⁶ Parched as burnt clay is my throat,
　　my tongue holds fast to my jaws.
　　You lay me in the dust of death.
¹⁷ For dogs have surrounded me;
　　a band of the wicked besets me.
　　They tear holes in my hands and my feet;

¹⁸ I can count every one of my bones.
　　They stare at me and gloat.
¹⁹ They divide my clothing among them,
　　casting lots for my robe.

²⁰ But you, O Lord, do not stay far off;
　　my strength, make haste to help me!
²¹ Rescue my soul from the sword,
　　my life from the grip of the dog.
²² Save my life from the jaws of the lion,
　　my poor soul from the horns of wild bulls.

²³ I will tell of your name to my kin,
 and praise you in the midst of the assembly:
²⁴ "You who fear the LORD, give praise;
 all offspring of Jacob, give glory;
 offer reverence, all you offspring of Israel.

²⁵ For the Almighty has never despised
 nor scorned the poverty of the poor.
 From the poor God's face is not hidden;
 they were heard whenever they cried."

²⁶ You are my praise in the great assembly.
 My vows I will pay before those who fear the Lord.
²⁷ The poor shall eat and shall have their fill.
 They shall praise the LORD, those who seek our
  God.
 May your hearts live on forever and ever!

28 All the earth shall remember and return to the
   Lord.
   All families of the nations worship and bow
   down,
29 for the kingdom is the Lord's, who is ruler of the
   nations.
30 They shall eat and adore, all who sleep in the
   earth;
   before the Lord shall bow all who go down to the
   dust.

31 And my soul shall live for God, my offspring too
   shall serve.
   To generations yet to come they shall tell of the
   Lord,
32 declare deliverance to peoples yet unborn:
   "These are the things the Lord has done."

Psalm 23 *(22)*

A Psalm of David.

The LORD is my shepherd;
there is nothing I shall want.
2 Fresh and green are the pastures
where you give me repose.
Near restful waters you lead me;
3 to revive my soul.

You guide me along the right path,
for the sake of your name.
4 Though I should walk in the valley of the shadow
of death,
no evil would I fear, for you are with me.
Your crook and your staff will give me comfort.

5 You have prepared a table before me
in the sight of my foes.
My head you have anointed with oil;
my cup is overflowing.

6 Surely goodness and kindness shall follow me
all the days of my life.
In the LORD's own house shall I dwell
for length of days unending.

Psalm 24 (23)

¹ *A Psalm of David.*

The LORD's is the earth and its fullness,
the world, and those who dwell in it.
² It is the Lord who set it on the seas,
and made it firm on the rivers.

³ Who shall climb the mountain of the LORD?
Who shall stand in God's holy place?
⁴ The clean of hands and pure of heart,
whose souls are not set on vain things,
who have not sworn deceitful words.

⁵ Blessings from the LORD shall they receive,
and right reward from the God who saves them.
⁶ Such are the people who seek the Lord,
who seek the face of the God of Jacob.

*   *   *

⁷ O gates, lift high your heads;
grow higher, ancient doors.
Let the king of glory enter!

⁸ Who is this king of glory?
  The LORD, the mighty, the valiant;
  the LORD, the valiant in war.

⁹ O gates, lift high your heads;
  grow higher, ancient doors.
  Let the king of glory enter!

¹⁰ Who is this king of glory?
  The LORD of heavenly hosts;
  this is the king of glory.

Psalm 25 *(24)*

¹ *Of David.*

  To you, O LORD, I lift up my soul.
² In you, O my God, I have trusted;
  let me not be put to shame;
  let not my enemies exult over me.
³ Let none who hope in you be put to shame;
  but shamed are those who wantonly break faith.

⁴ O LORD, make me know your ways.
  Teach me your paths.
⁵ Guide me in your truth, and teach me;
  for you are the God of my salvation.
  I have hoped in you all day long

⁶ Remember your compassion, O Lord,
   and your gracious love,
   for they are from of old.

⁷ Do not remember the sins of my youth,
   nor my transgressions.
   In your gracious love remember me,
   because of your goodness, O Lord.

⁸ Good and upright is the Lord,
   who therefore shows the way to sinners,
⁹ who guides the humble in right judgment;
   who teaches God's way to the humble.

¹⁰ All the paths of the Lord are gracious love and
       faithfulness,
   for those who keep the commands of the
       covenant.
¹¹ O Lord, for the sake of your name,
   forgive my guilt, for it is great.

¹² Who are they that fear the Lord?
   God will show them the path to choose.
¹³ Their souls shall live in happiness,
   and their descendants shall possess the land.
¹⁴ The friendship of the Lord is for those who fear
       God;
   to them is revealed the covenant.

15 My eyes are always on the LORD,
   who rescues my feet from the snare.
16 Turn to me and have mercy on me,
   for I am alone and poor.

17 Relieve the anguish of my heart,
   and set me free from my distress.
18 See my lowliness and suffering,
   and take away all my sins.

19 See how many are my foes:
   with a violent hatred they hate me.
20 Preserve my life and rescue me.
   Let me not be put to shame,
   for in you I take refuge.

21 May integrity and virtue protect me,
   for I have hoped in you, O LORD.
22 Grant redemption to Israel, O God,
   from all its distress.

Psalm 26 (25)

¹ *Of David.*

Give judgment for me, O Lᴏʀᴅ,
for I have walked in my integrity.
I have trusted in the Lᴏʀᴅ; I have not wavered.

² Examine me, Lᴏʀᴅ, and try me.
O test my heart and my mind.
³ Your faithful love is before my eyes,
and I walk according to your truth.

⁴ I never take my seat with liars,
and with hypocrites I shall not go.
⁵ I hate the evildoer's company;
I will not take my seat with the wicked.

⁶ I wash my hands in innocence
and take my place around your altar,
⁷ singing a song of thanksgiving,
recounting all your wonders.
⁸ O Lᴏʀᴅ, I love the house where you dwell,
the place where your glory abides.

⁹ Do not sweep away my soul with sinners,
    nor my life with those who shed blood,
¹⁰ in whose hands are evil plots,
    whose right hands are filled with a bribe.

¹¹ As for me, I walk in my integrity.
    Redeem me and have mercy on me.
¹² My foot stands on level ground:
    I will bless the Lord in the assembly.

Psalm 27 (26)

[1] *Of David.*

The LORD is my light and my salvation;
whom shall I fear?
The LORD is the stronghold of my life;
whom should I dread?

[2] When those who do evil draw near
to devour my flesh,
it is they, my enemies and foes,
who stumble and fall.

[3] Though an army encamp against me,
my heart would not fear.
Though war break out against me,
even then would I trust.

[4] There is one thing I ask of the LORD,
only this do I seek:
to live in the house of the LORD
all the days of my life,
to gaze on the beauty of the LORD,
to inquire at his temple.

[5] For there I am safely sheltered
in the day of evil;
God hides me under cover of a tent;
setting me high upon a rock.

⁶ And now my head shall be raised
   above my foes who surround me,
   and I shall offer within God's tent
   sacrifices full of exultation.
   I will sing and make music for the LORD.

⁷ O LORD, hear my voice when I call;
   have mercy and answer me.
⁸ Of you my heart has spoken,
   "Seek the face of God."

   It is your face, O LORD, that I seek;
⁹ hide not your face from me.
   Dismiss not your servant in anger;
   you have been my help.

   Do not abandon or forsake me,
   O God, my Savior!
¹⁰ Though father and mother forsake me,
    the LORD will receive me.

¹¹ Instruct me, LORD, in your way;
    on an even path lead me
    because of my enemies.
¹² Do not leave me to the will of my foes,
    for false witnesses rise up against me,
    and they breathe out violence.

¹³ I believe I shall see the goodness of the LORD
    in the land of the living.
¹⁴ Wait for the LORD; be strong;
    be stouthearted, and wait for the LORD!

Psalm 28 (27)

¹ *Of David.*

To you, O LORD, I call;
my rock, be not deaf to me.
I shall go down to those in the pit,
if you are silent to me.

² Hear the voice of my pleading
as I call to you for help,
as I lift up my hands in prayer
to your holy place.

³ Do not drag me away with the wicked,
with those who do evil,
who speak words of peace to their neighbors,
but with malice in their hearts.

⁴ Repay them according to their deeds,
according to the evil of their actions.
According to their handiwork, repay them;
render them their due reward.

⁵ For they ignore your deeds, O LORD,
  and the work of your hands.
  May you ruin them and never rebuild them.
⁶ Blest be the LORD, who has heard
  the sound of my appeal.

⁷ The LORD is my strength and my shield;
  in God my heart trusts.
  I was helped; my heart rejoices,
  and I praise God with my song.

⁸ The LORD is the strength of the people,
  a saving refuge for God's anointed.
⁹ Save your people and bless your heritage.
  Shepherd them and carry them forever.

Psalm 29 (28)

Ascribe to the LORD, you heavenly powers,
  ascribe to the LORD glory and strength.
² Ascribe to the LORD the glory of God's name;
  bow down before the LORD, majestic in holiness.

³ The voice of the LORD upon the waters,
  the God of glory thunders;
  the LORD on the immensity of waters;
⁴ the voice of the LORD full of power;
  the voice of the LORD full of splendor.

⁵ The voice of the LORD shatters cedars,
  the LORD shatters the cedars of Lebanon,
⁶ making Lebanon leap like a calf,
  and Sirion like a young wild ox.

⁷ The voice of the LORD flashes flames of fire.
⁸ The voice of the LORD shakes the wilderness,
  the LORD shakes the wilderness of Kadesh;
⁹ the voice of the LORD rends the oak tree
  and strips the forest bare.
  In God's temple they all cry, "Glory!"

¹⁰ The LORD sits enthroned above the flood;
  the LORD sits as king forever.
¹¹ Give strength to your people, O LORD.
  O LORD, bless your people with peace.

Psalm 30 (29)

¹ *A Psalm. A Canticle for the Dedication of the Temple. Of David.*

² I will extol you, Lᴏʀᴅ, for you have raised me up,
   and have not let my enemies rejoice over me.

³ O Lᴏʀᴅ my God, I cried to you for help,
   and you have healed me.
⁴ O Lᴏʀᴅ, you have lifted up my soul from Sheol,
   restored me to life from those who sink into the
      pit.

⁵ Sing psalms to the Lᴏʀᴅ, you faithful ones;
   give thanks to God's holy name.
⁶ Divine anger lasts a moment, but favor all
      through life.
   At night come tears, but dawn brings joy.

⁷ I said to myself in my good fortune:
   "I shall never be shaken."
⁸ O Lᴏʀᴅ, your favor had set me like a mountain
      stronghold.
   Then you hid your face, and I was put to
      confusion.

⁹ To you, O LORD, I cried,
    to my Lord I appealed for mercy:
¹⁰ "What profit is my lifeblood, my going to the
       grave?
    Can dust give you thanks, or proclaim your
       faithfulness?"

¹¹ Hear, O LORD, and have mercy on me;
    be my helper, O LORD.
¹² You have changed my mourning into dancing,
    removed my sackcloth and girded me with joy.
¹³ So let my soul sing psalms to you and not be
       silent.
    O LORD my God, I will thank you forever.

Psalm 31 (30)

¹ *For the Choirmaster. A Psalm of David.*

² In you, O Lord, I take refuge.
  Let me never be put to shame.
  In your righteousness, set me free;
³ incline your ear to me, and speedily rescue me.

  Be a rock of refuge for me,
  a mighty stronghold to save me.
⁴ For you are my rock, my stronghold!
  Lead me, guide me, for the sake of your name.

⁵ Release me from the snare they have hidden,
  for you indeed are my refuge.
⁶ Into your hands I commend my spirit.
  You will redeem me, O Lord, O faithful God.

⁷ You detest those who serve empty idols.
  As for me, I trust in the Lord.

⁸ Let me be glad and rejoice in your love,
  for you who have seen my affliction
  and taken heed of my soul's distress,
⁹ have not left me in the hands of the enemy,
  but set my feet at large.

¹⁰ Have mercy on me, O LORD,
    for I am in distress.
    My eyes are wasted away with grief,
    as are my soul and my body.

¹¹ For my life is spent with sorrow,
    and my years with sighs.
    Affliction has broken down my strength,
    and my bones waste away.

¹² Because of all my foes
    I have become a reproach,
    an object of scorn to my neighbors
    and of fear to my friends.

    Those who see me in the street, they flee from me.
¹³ I am forgotten, like someone dead,
    and have become like a broken vessel.

¹⁴ I have heard the slander of the crowd;
    terror all around me,
    as they plot together against me,
    as they plan to take my life.

¹⁵ But as for me, I trust in you, O LORD;
    I say, "You are my God.
¹⁶ There in your hands is my lot;
    from the hands of my enemies deliver me,
    and from those who pursue me.

¹⁷ "Let your face shine on your servant.
   Save me in your faithful love.
¹⁸ Let me not be put to shame, O LORD,
   for I call on you;
   Let the wicked be shamed!
   Let them be silenced in Sheol!

¹⁹ "Let lying lips be stilled,
   that speak haughtily against the righteous
   with pride and contempt."

²⁰ How great is the goodness, LORD,
   that you keep for those who fear you,
   that you show to those who trust you
   in the sight of the children of Adam.

²¹ You hide them in the shelter of your presence,
   secure from human scheming;
   you keep them safe within your tent
   from disputing tongues.

²² Blest be the LORD who has wondrously shown me
   faithful love in a fortified city!

²³ "I am far removed from your sight,"
   I said in my alarm.
   Yet you heard the voice of my plea
   when I cried to you for help.

²⁴ Love the LORD, all you his saints.
   The LORD guards the faithful.
   But the LORD will repay to the full
   the one who acts with pride.
²⁵ Be strong, let your heart take courage,
   all who hope in the LORD.

Psalm 32 (31)

[1] *Of David. A Maskil.*

Blessed is one whose transgression is forgiven,
whose sin is remitted.
[2] Blessed the one to whom the LORD imputes no
guilt,
in whose spirit is no guile.

[3] I kept it secret and my frame was wasted.
I groaned all day long,
[4] For your hand, by day and by night,
lay heavy upon me.
Indeed, my strength was dried up
as by the summer's heat.

[5] To you I have acknowledged my sin;
my guilt I did not hide.
I said, "I will confess my transgression to the
LORD."
And you have forgiven the guilt of my sin.

[6] So let each faithful one pray to you
in the time of need.
The floods of water may reach high,
but such a one they shall not reach.

⁷ You are a hiding place for me;
  you keep me safe from distress;
  you surround me with cries of deliverance.

⁸ I will instruct you and teach you
  the way you should go;
  I will fix my eyes upon you.

⁹ Be not like horse and mule, unintelligent,
  needing bridle and bit,
  or else they will not approach you.

¹⁰ Many sorrows has the wicked,
   but loving kindness surrounds the one who trusts
      in the LORD.

¹¹ Rejoice in the LORD, exult you righteous!
   Ring out your joy, all you upright of heart!

Psalm 33 (32)

1 Ring out your joy to the LORD, O you righteous;
for praise is fitting from the upright.
2 Give thanks to the LORD upon the harp;
with a ten-stringed lute sing songs to God.
3 O sing a song that is new;
play skillfully, with shouts of joy.

4 For the word of the LORD is upright,
and all God's works to be trusted.
5 The LORD loves justice and right;
God's faithful love fills the earth.

6 By the word of the LORD the heavens were made,
by the breath of God's mouth, all their host.
7 As in a flask, God collects the waves of the ocean,
and stores up the depths of the sea.

8 Let all the earth fear the LORD,
all who live in the world show reverence.
9 God spoke, and it came to be;
commanded and it stood in place.

10 The LORD frustrates the designs of the nations,
and defeats the plans of the peoples.
11 The designs of the LORD stand forever,
the plans of God's heart from age to age.

¹² Blessed the nation whose God is the LORD,
the people God has chosen as a heritage.
¹³ From the heavens the LORD looks forth,
and sees the whole human race.

¹⁴ From the heavenly dwelling God gazes
on all the dwellers on the earth,
¹⁵ God who shapes the hearts of them all,
and considers all their deeds.

¹⁶ A ruler is not saved by a great army,
nor a warrior preserved by great strength.
¹⁷ A vain hope for safety is the horse;
despite its power it cannot save.

¹⁸ Behold, the eyes of the LORD
are on those who fear him,
who hope in God's faithful love,
¹⁹ to rescue their soul from death,
to keep them alive in famine.

²⁰ Our soul is waiting for the LORD,
our God, our help and our shield.
²¹ In you do our hearts find joy;
we trust in your holy name.
²² May your faithful love be upon us,
as we hope in you, O LORD.

Psalm 34 *(33)*

¹ *Of David, when he feigned madness before*
   Abimelech, so that he drove him out,
   and he went away.

² I will bless the Lord at all times;
   praise is always in my mouth.
³ In the Lord my soul shall make its boast;
   the humble shall hear and be glad.

⁴ Glorify the Lord with me;
   together let us praise God's name.
⁵ I sought the Lord, who answered me,
   and set me free from all my terrors.

⁶ Look towards the Lord and be radiant;
   let your faces not be abashed.
⁷ When the lowly call out, the Lord hears,
   and rescues them from all their distress.

⁸ The angel of the Lord is encamped
   around those who are reverent, to rescue them.
⁹ Taste and see that the Lord is good.
   Blessed are they who seek refuge in him.

¹⁰ Fear the Lord, you holy ones.
   They lack nothing, those who fear God.
¹¹ The rich suffer want and go hungry,
   but those who seek the Lord lack no blessing.

¹² Come, children, and hear me,
   that I may teach you the fear of the LORD.
¹³ Who is eager for life
   and longs to see prosperous days?

¹⁴ Guard your tongue from evil,
   and your lips from speaking deceit.
¹⁵ Turn aside from evil and do good.
   Seek after peace, and pursue it.

¹⁶ The eyes of the LORD are on the righteous;
   God's ears are open to their cry.
¹⁷ The LORD's face is turned against the wicked
   to cut off their remembrance from the earth.

¹⁸ When the righteous cry out, the LORD hears,
   and rescues them in all their distress.
¹⁹ The LORD is close to the brokenhearted,
   and saves those whose spirit is crushed.

²⁰ Many are the trials of the righteous,
   but from them all the LORD will rescue them,
²¹ God keeps guard over all their bones;
   not one of their bones shall be broken.

²² Evil brings death to the wicked;
   those who hate the righteous are doomed.
²³ The souls of those who serve the LORD are
       ransomed.
   None who trust in God shall be condemned.

Psalm 35 (34)

¹ *Of David.*

Contend, O LORD, with my contenders;
fight those who fight me.
² Take up your buckler and shield;
arise in my defense.

³ Take up the javelin and the spear
against those who pursue me.
Say to my soul, "I am your salvation."

⁴ Let those who seek my life
be shamed and disgraced.
Let those who plan evil against me
be routed in confusion.

⁵ Let them be like chaff before the wind;
let the angel of the LORD drive them on.
⁶ Let their path be slippery and dark;
let the angel of the LORD pursue them.

⁷ Unprovoked, they have hidden a net for me;
unprovoked, they have dug a pit for me.
⁸ Let ruin fall upon them,
and take them by surprise.
Let them be caught in the net they have hidden;
let them fall in their own pit.

⁹ Then my soul shall rejoice in the LORD,
   and exult in God's salvation.
¹⁰ All my bones will say,
   "LORD, who is like you
   who rescue the weak from the strong
   and the poor from the oppressor?"

¹¹ Lying witnesses arise,
   asking me questions I cannot understand.
¹² They repay me evil for good;
   my soul is forlorn.

¹³ When they were sick I dressed in sackcloth,
   afflicted my soul with fasting,
   and with prayer ever new in my heart,
¹⁴ as for a brother, a friend.
   I went as though mourning a mother,
   bowed down with grief.

¹⁵ Now that I stumble, they gladly gather;
   they gather, and mock me.
   I myself do not know them,
   yet strangers tear at me ceaselessly.
¹⁶ They provoke me with mockery on mockery,
   and gnash their teeth at me.

¹⁷ O Lord, how long will you look on?
  Rescue my life from their ravages,
  my soul from these lions.
¹⁸ Then I will thank you in the great assembly;
  amid the mighty throng I will praise you.

¹⁹ Do not let my lying foes
  rejoice over me.
  Do not let those who hate me without cause
  wink eyes at each other.

²⁰ For they do not speak of peace,
  but against the quiet in the land
  they conceive deceitful words,
²¹ and, with mouths wide open,
  they utter their cry against me:
  "Yes, yes! Our eyes have seen it!"

²² O Lord, you have seen; do not be silent;
  Lord, do not stand far off!
²³ Awake! And stir to my defense,
  to my cause, O my God and my Lord!

²⁴ Vindicate me, Lord, my God,
  in accord with your righteousness;
  and let them not rejoice over me.

²⁵ Do not let them think in their hearts,
   "Yes, we have won."
   Do not let them say,
   "We have destroyed you!"

²⁶ Let them be shamed and brought to disgrace
   who rejoice at my misfortune.
   Let them be covered with shame and confusion
   who raise themselves against me.

²⁷ Let them exult and be glad
   who delight in my deliverance.
   Let them say without end,
   "Great is the Lord who delights
   in the peace of this servant."

²⁸ Then my tongue shall speak of your righteousness,
   and all day long of your praise.

Psalm 36 *(35)*

¹ *For the Choirmaster. Of David, the servant of the* Lord.

² Transgression speaks to sinners
in the depths of their hearts.
There is no fear of God before their eyes.

³ In their own eyes, they flatter themselves;
they do not see and detest their own guilt.
⁴ The words of their mouths are mischief and
deceit.
They have ceased to be prudent and do good.

⁵ On their beds they plot iniquity.
They set their feet on every wicked way;
no evil do they reject.

⁶ Your faithful love, O Lord, reaches to heaven,
your truth to the clouds.
⁷ Your righteousness is like the mountains of God;
like the great deep, your justice.
Both human being and beast you save, O Lord.

8 How precious is your love, O God!
   The children of Adam seek shelter
   in the shadow of your wings.

9 They feast on the riches of your house;
   you give them drink from the stream of your
      delight.
10 For with you is the fountain of life,
   and in your light we see light.

11 Maintain your love for those who know you,
   your saving justice to upright hearts.
12 Let the foot of the proud not tread on me
   nor the hand of the wicked drive me out.
13 There have the evildoers fallen;
   flung down, unable to rise!

Psalm 37 (36)

    Do not fret because of the wicked;
      do not envy those who do evil,
² for they wither quickly like grass
      and fade like the green of the fields.

³ Trust in the LORD and do good;
      then you will dwell in the land and find safe
         pasture.
⁴ Find your delight in the LORD,
      who grants your heart's desire.

⁵ Commit your way to the LORD;
      if you trust, then God will act,
⁶ and make your righteousness shine like the light,
      your justice like the noonday sun.

⁷ Be still before the LORD and wait in patience;
      do not fret at the one who prospers,
      the one who makes evil plots.

⁸ Calm your anger and forget your rage;
      do not fret, it only leads to evil.
⁹ For those who do evil shall perish.
      But those who hope in the LORD,
      they shall inherit the land.

¹⁰ A little longer–and the wicked are gone.
   Look at their place: they are not there.
¹¹ But the meek shall inherit the land
   and delight in fullness of peace.

¹² The wicked plot against the righteous
   and gnash their teeth against them;
¹³ but the LORD will laugh at the wicked,
   seeing that their day is at hand.

¹⁴ The wicked draw the sword, bend their bows,
   to slaughter the poor and needy,
   to slay those whose ways are upright.
¹⁵ Their sword shall pierce their own hearts,
   and their bows shall be broken to pieces.

¹⁶ How much better the little of the righteous,
   than the overflowing wealth of the wicked;
¹⁷ for the arms of the wicked shall be broken,
   and the LORD will support the righteous.

¹⁸ The LORD takes note of the days of the blameless;
   their heritage will last forever.
¹⁹ They shall not be put to shame in evil days;
   in time of famine they shall have their fill.

²⁰ But all the wicked shall perish;
   the enemies of the LORD shall be consumed.
   They are like the beauty of the meadows;
   they shall vanish, they shall vanish like smoke.

²¹ The wicked borrows and does not repay,
but the righteous is generous and gives.
²² Those blessed by God shall inherit the land,
while those who are cursed shall be cut off.

²³ By the LORD are the steps of a warrior
made firm in delight of God's ways.
²⁴ Though they stumble they shall never fall,
for the LORD will hold them by the hand.

²⁵ I was young and now I am old,
but I have never seen the righteous forsaken
nor their children begging for bread.
²⁶ All the day they are generous and lend,
and their children become a blessing.

²⁷ Then turn away from evil and do good,
and you may abide forever;
²⁸ for indeed, the LORD loves justice,
and will never forsake the faithful.

The unjust shall be wiped out forever,
and the descendants of the wicked cut off.
²⁹ The righteous shall inherit the land;
there they shall abide forever.

³⁰ The mouths of the righteous utter wisdom,
and their tongues tell forth what is just.
³¹ The law of God is in their hearts;
their steps shall be saved from stumbling.

³² The wicked keep watch for the righteous,
  and seek an occasion to destroy them.
³³ The LORD will not leave them in their power,
  nor let them be condemned when they are
      judged.

³⁴ Then wait for the LORD, keep to the way.
  God will exalt you to inherit the land,
  and you will see the wicked cut off.

³⁵ I have seen the wicked triumphant,
  towering like cedars of Lebanon.
³⁶ I passed by again; they were gone.
  I searched; they were nowhere to be found.

³⁷ Mark the blameless, observe the upright;
  for the peaceful a future lies in store,
³⁸ but sinners shall all be destroyed,
  the future of the wicked cut off.

³⁹ But from the LORD comes the salvation of the
      righteous,
  their stronghold in time of distress.
⁴⁰ The LORD helps them and rescues them,
  rescues and saves them from the wicked,
  for their refuge is in God.

Psalm 38 *(37)*

¹ *A Psalm of David. For a Memorial.*

² O LORD, do not rebuke me in your anger;
   reprove me not in your rage.
³ For your arrows have sunk deep in me;
   your hand has come down upon me.

⁴ There is no soundness in my flesh because of your
       anger:
   There is no health in my bones because of my sin.

⁵ My guilt towers higher than my head;
   it is a weight too heavy to bear.
⁶ My wounds are foul and festering,
   the result of my own folly.
⁷ I am bowed and brought to my knees.
   I go mourning all the day long.

⁸ All my frame is burning with fever;
   there is no soundness in my flesh.
⁹ I am spent and utterly crushed,
   I cry aloud in anguish of heart.

¹⁰ O Lord, all my longing lies before you;
    my groans are not hidden from you.
¹¹ My heart throbs, my strength is spent;
    the very light has gone from my eyes.

12 Friends and companions stand aloof from my
      illness;
   those closest to me stand far off.
13 Those who plot against my life lay snares;
   those who seek my ruin speak of harm,
   planning treachery all the day long.

14 But I, like someone deaf, do not hear;
   like someone mute, I do not open my mouth.
15 I am like one who hears nothing,
   in whose mouth is no defense.

16 But for you, O LORD, I wait;
   it is you, LORD my God, who will answer.
17 I pray, "Let them not gloat over me,
   exult if my foot should slip."

18 For I am on the point of falling,
   and my pain is always with me.
19 I confess that I am guilty;
   and I am grieved because of my sin.

20 My enemies live on and grow strong,
   and many hate me without cause.
21 They repay me evil for good,
   and attack me for seeking what is good.

22 Forsake me not, O LORD!
   My God, be not far from me!
23 Make haste and come to my help,
   my Lord and my salvation!

Psalm 39 (38)

¹ *For the Choirmaster, for Jeduthun. A Psalm of David.*

² I said, "I will be watchful of my ways,
   for fear I should sin with my tongue.
   I will put a curb on my lips
   when the wicked stand before me."
³ I was mute, silent, very still,
   as my pain became intense.

⁴ My heart was burning within me.
   With these thoughts, the fire blazed up,
   and my tongue burst forth into speech:
⁵ "O LORD, you have shown me my end,
   how short is the length of my days.
   Now I know how fleeting is my life.

⁶ "How short the span of days you have given me;
   my life is as nothing in your sight.
   Surely all people stand as but a breath.
⁷ Surely each of us lives as a shadow,
   surely stored riches are as a mere breath;
   we do not know who will gather them."

⁸ And now, Lord, what is there to wait for?
  In you rests all my hope.
⁹ Set me free from all my sins,
  do not make me the taunt of the fool.
¹⁰ I was silent, not opening my lips,
  because this was all your doing.

¹¹ Take away your scourge from me.
  I am crushed by the blows of your hand.
¹² You chastise us, sinners, with due punishment;
  like a moth you devour all we treasure.
  We are all of us no more than a breath.

¹³ O LORD, give heed to my prayer;
  turn your ear to my cry;
  do not be deaf to my weeping.
  Behold, I am a stranger to you,
  a pilgrim, like all my forebears.

¹⁴ Look away from me that I may smile
  before I depart to be no more.

Psalm 40 (39)

¹ *For the Choirmaster. Of David. A Psalm.*

² I waited, I waited for the LORD,
  and God stooped down to me,
  having heard my cry.

³ The Lord drew me from the deadly pit,
  from the miry clay.
  God set my feet upon a rock,
  made my footsteps firm.

⁴ The Lord put a new song into my mouth,
  praise of our God.
  Many shall see and fear
  and shall trust in the LORD.

⁵ Blessed are they who have placed
  their trust in the LORD,
  and do not turn to the proud
  who follow false gods.

⁶ How many are the wonders and designs
  that you have worked for us, O LORD my God;
  you have no equal.
  Should I wish to proclaim or speak of them,
  they would be more than I can tell!

⁷ You delight not in sacrifice and offering,
   but in an open ear.
   You do not ask for holocaust and sin offering.

⁸ Then I said, "Behold, I have come."
   In the scroll of the book it stands written of me:
⁹ "I delight to do your will, O my God;
   your instruction lies deep within me."

¹⁰ Your righteousness I have proclaimed
    in the great assembly.
    My lips I have not sealed;
    you know it, O LORD.

¹¹ Your saving help I have not hidden in my heart;
    of your faithful salvation I have spoken.
    I made no secret of your gracious love
    and your truth to the great assembly.

¹² You, O LORD, will not withhold your
               compassion from me.
    Your loving kindness and your faithfulness will
               always guard me.

¹³ For I am beset with evils
    too many to be counted.
    My iniquities have overtaken me,
    till I can see no more.
    They are more than the hairs of my head,
    and my heart is sinking.

¹⁴ Be pleased, O LORD, to rescue me;
   LORD, make haste to help me.
¹⁵ O let there be shame and confusion
   on those who seek my life.

   O let them turn back in confusion
   who delight in my harm.
¹⁶ Let them be appalled because of their shame,
   those who jeer and mock me.

¹⁷ O let there be rejoicing and gladness
   for all who seek you.
   Let them ever say, "The LORD is great,"
   who long for your salvation.

¹⁸ Wretched and poor though I am,
   the Lord is mindful of me.
   You are my rescuer, my help;
   O my God, do not delay.

Psalm 41 (40)

¹ *For the Choirmaster. A Psalm of David.*

² Blessed are they who have concern for the poor.
   In time of trouble, the LORD will rescue them.

³ The LORD will guard them, preserve their life,
   and make them blessed in the land,
   not give them up to the will of their foes.

⁴ The LORD will help them on their bed of pain;
  in their sickness, you tend even to their bedding.

⁵ As for me, I said, "LORD, have mercy on me;
  heal my soul, for I have sinned against you."
⁶ My foes speak evil against me and wonder,
  how long before I die and my name is forgotten?
⁷ When they come to visit me, they speak empty
      words.
  Their hearts store up malice; on leaving, they
      spread lies.

⁸ All my foes whisper together against me.
  They devise evil plots against me,
⁹ Saying something deadly has fastened upon me,
  that I will not rise from where I lie.

¹⁰ Thus even my friend, in whom I trusted,
  who ate my bread,
  has lifted a heel against me.

¹¹ But you, O LORD, have mercy on me.
  Raise me up and I will repay them.
¹² By this I know your favor:
  that my foes do not triumph over me.
¹³ In my integrity you have upheld me,
  and have set me in your presence forever.

*   *   *

[14] Blest be the LORD, the God of Israel,
  from age to age. Amen. Amen.

BOOK TWO
OF THE PSALTER

Psalm 42 (41)

¹ *For the Choirmaster. A* Maskil. *Of the sons of Korah.*

² Like the deer that yearns for running streams,
so my soul is yearning for you, my God.

³ My soul is thirsting for God, the living God;
when can I enter and appear before the face of
God?

⁴ My tears have become my bread,
by day, by night,
as they say to me all the day long,
"Where is your God?"

⁵ These things will I remember as I pour out my
soul:
for I would go to the place of your wondrous
tent,
all the way to the house of God,
amid cries of gladness and thanksgiving,
the throng keeping joyful festival.

⁶ Why are you cast down, my soul;
why groan within me?
Hope in God, whom I will praise yet again,
my saving presence and my God.

7 My soul is cast down within me,
   therefore I remember you
   from the land of Jordan and Mount Hermon,
   from the Hill of Mizar.

8 Deep is calling on deep,
   in the roar of your torrents;
   your billows and all your waves
   swept over me.

9 By day the LORD decrees loving mercy;
   by night a song is with me,
   a prayer to the God of my life.

10 I will say to God, my rock,
   "Why have you forgotten me?
   Why do I go mourning
   oppressed by the foe?"

11 With a deadly wound in my bones,
   my enemies revile me,
   saying to me all the day long,
   "Where is your God?"

12 Why are you cast down, my soul;
   why groan within me?
   Hope in God, whom I will praise yet again,
   my saving presence and my God.

Psalm 43 (42)

¹ Give me justice, O God, and plead my cause
  against a nation that is faithless.
  From those who are deceitful and cunning
  rescue me, O God.

² You, O God, are my strength;
  why have you rejected me?
  Why do I go mourning,
  oppressed by the foe?

³ O send forth your light and your truth;
  they will guide me on.
  They will bring me to your holy mountain,
  to the place where you dwell.

⁴ And I will come to the altar of God,
  to God, my joy and gladness.
  To you will I give thanks on the harp,
  O God, my God.

⁵ Why are you cast down, my soul;
  why groan within me?
  Hope in God, whom I will praise yet again,
  my saving presence and my God.

Psalm 44 (43)

¹ *For the Choirmaster. Of the sons of Korah.*
   A Maskil.

² We heard with our own ears, O God;
   our forebears have declared to us
   the deeds you did in their days,
   you yourself, in days long ago.

³ With your own hand you drove out the nations,
   but them you planted;
   You brought affliction on the peoples;
   but them you set free.

⁴ No sword of their own won the land;
   no arm of their own brought them victory.
   It was your right hand and your arm,
   and the light of your face, for you loved them.

⁵ You are my ruler, O God;
   you command the victories for Jacob.
⁶ Through you we beat down our foes;
   in your name we trampled our aggressors.

⁷ For it was not in my bow that I trusted,
   nor yet was I saved by my sword:
⁸ it was you who saved us from our foes;
   those who hate us, you put to shame.
⁹ All day long our boast was in God,
   and we will praise your name forever.

¹⁰ Yet now you have rejected us, disgraced us;
   you no longer go forth with our armies.
¹¹ You make us retreat from the foe;
   those who hate us plunder us at will.

¹² You make us like sheep for the slaughter,
   and scatter us among the nations.
¹³ You sell your own people for nothing,
   and make no profit by the sale.

¹⁴ You make us the taunt of our neighbors,
   the mockery and scorn of those around us.
¹⁵ Among the nations you make us a byword;
   among the peoples they shake their heads.

¹⁶ All day long my disgrace is before me;
   my face is covered with shame
¹⁷ at the voice of the taunter, the scoffer,
   at the sight of the foe and avenger.

¹⁸ This befell us though we had not forgotten you;
  we were not false to your covenant.
¹⁹ We had not withdrawn our hearts;
  our feet had not strayed from your path.
²⁰ Yet you have crushed us in a haunt of jackals,
  and overwhelmed us with the shadow of death.

²¹ Had we forgotten the name of our God,
  or stretched out our hands to a strange god,
²² would not God have found this out,
  who knows the secrets of the heart?
²³ It is for you we are slain all day long,
  and are counted as sheep for the slaughter.

²⁴ Awake, O Lord! Why do you sleep?
  Arise! Do not reject us forever.
²⁵ Why do you hide your face,
  and forget our oppression and misery?

²⁶ For our soul is brought low to the dust;
  our body lies prostrate on the earth.
²⁷ Stand up and come to our help!
  Redeem us with your merciful love!

Psalm 45 (44)

¹ *For the Choirmaster. Intoned like "The Lilies."*
   Of the sons of Korah. A Maskil. *A Love Song.*

² My heart overflows with noble words.
   To the king I address the song I have made,
   my tongue as nimble as the pen of a scribe.

³ You are the most handsome of the sons of men,
   and graciousness is poured out upon your lips,
   for God has blessed you forevermore.

⁴ Gird your sword upon your thigh, O mighty one,
   with your splendor and your majesty.
⁵ In your majesty ride on in triumph
   for the cause of faithfulness and clemency and
      righteousness.
   May your right hand show your wondrous deeds.

⁶ Your arrows are sharp
   in the heart of the foes of the king.
   Peoples fall beneath you.

⁷ Your throne, O God, shall endure forever.
   A scepter of justice is the scepter of your kingdom.
⁸ Your love is for righteousness; your hatred for evil.

Therefore God, your God, has anointed you
  with the oil of gladness above your companions:
⁹ all your robes are fragrant with aloes, myrrh, and
    cassia.

From the ivory palace you are gladdened with
    music.
¹⁰ The daughters of kings are those whom you favor.
  At your right stands the queen in gold of Ophir.

¹¹ Listen, O daughter; pay heed and give ear:
  forget your own people and your father's house.
¹² So will the king desire your beauty.
  He is your lord, pay homage to him.
¹³ And the daughter of Tyre shall come with gifts;
  the richest of the people shall seek your favor.

¹⁴ The daughter of the king is clothed with
    splendor;
  her robes are threaded with gold.
¹⁵ In fine clothing she is led to the king;
  behind her, her maiden companions follow.
¹⁶ They are escorted amid gladness and joy;
  they pass within the palace of the king.

¹⁷ Sons will be yours to succeed your fathers;
  you will make them rulers over all the earth.
¹⁸ I will make your name forever remembered.
  Thus the peoples will praise you from age to age.

Psalm 46 *(45)*

¹ *For the Choirmaster. Of the sons of Korah. Intoned*
  like "The Maidens." A Song.

² God is for us a refuge and strength,
  an ever-present help in time of distress:
³ so we shall not fear though the earth should rock,
  though the mountains quake to the heart of the
    sea;
⁴ even though its waters rage and foam,
  even though the mountains be shaken by its
    tumult.

  The LORD of hosts is with us:
  the God of Jacob is our stronghold.

⁵ The waters of a river give joy to God's city,
  the holy place, the abode of the Most High.
⁶ God is within her, she cannot be shaken;
  God will help her at the dawning of the day.
⁷ Nations are in tumult, kingdoms are shaken:
  a divine voice roars, and the earth melts away.

⁸ The LORD of hosts is with us:
  the God of Jacob is our stronghold.

9 Come and behold the works of the LORD,
   the awesome deeds God has done on the earth.
10 God puts an end to wars over all the earth;
   breaking bows, snapping spears, and burning
         shields with fire:
11 "Be still and know that I am God,
   exalted over nations, exalted over earth!"

12 The LORD of hosts is with us:
   the God of Jacob is our stronghold.

Psalm 47 (46)

¹ For the Choirmaster. Of the sons of Korah. A Psalm.

² All peoples, clap your hands.
   Cry to God with shouts of joy!
³ For the LORD, the Most High, is awesome,
   the great king over all the earth.

⁴ God humbles peoples under us
   and nations under our feet.
⁵ Our heritage God chose for us,
   the pride of Jacob the beloved.

⁶ God has gone up with shouts of joy.
   The LORD goes up with trumpet blast.
⁷ Sing praise for God; sing praise!
   Sing praise to our king; sing praise!
⁸ For God is king of all the earth.
   Sing praise with a hymn.

⁹ God is reigning over nations,
   God sits upon a holy throne.
¹⁰ The leaders of the peoples are assembled
   with the people of the God of Abraham.
   For the rulers of the earth belong to God,
   who is greatly exalted.

Psalm 48 *(47)*

¹ *A Song. A Psalm. Of the sons of Korah.*

² Great is the LORD and highly to be praised
  in the city of our God,
³ whose holy mountain rises in beauty,
  the joy of all the earth.

  Mount Zion, in the heart of the North,
  the city of the Mighty King!
⁴ God, in the midst of her citadels,
  is shown to be her stronghold.

⁵ Behold! the kings assembled;
  together they advanced.
⁶ They saw; at once they marveled;
  dismayed, they fled in fear.

⁷ A trembling seized them there,
  anguish, like pangs in giving birth,
⁸ As when the east wind shatters
  the ships of Tarshish.

⁹ As we have heard, so we have seen
  in the city of our God,
  in the city of the LORD of hosts,
  which God establishes forever.

¹⁰ Your faithful love, O God,
   we ponder in your temple.
¹¹ Your praise, O God, like your name,
   reaches the ends of the earth.

   Your right hand is filled with saving justice.
¹² Mount Zion rejoices.
   The daughters of Judah rejoice
   at the sight of your judgments.

¹³ Walk through Zion, walk all around her;
   count the number of her towers.
¹⁴ Consider all her ramparts;
   examine her castles,

   That you may tell the next generation
¹⁵ that such is our God,
   Our God forever and always,
   who will guide us forever.

Psalm 49 (48)

1 For the Choirmaster. Of the sons of Korah. A Psalm.

2 Hear this, all you peoples,
   give ear, all who dwell in the world,
3 people both high and low,
   rich and poor alike!

4 My mouth will utter wisdom.
   The reflections of my heart offer insight.
5 I will incline my ear to a mystery;
   with the harp I will set forth my problem.

6 Why should I fear in evil days
   the malice of the foes who surround me,
7 those who trust in their wealth,
   and boast of the vastness of their riches?

8 No one can ransom a brother or a sister,
   nor pay a price to God for a life.
9 How high is the price of a soul!
   The ransom can never be enough!
10 No one can buy life unending,
   nor avoid going down to the pit.

11 We see that the wise will die;
    the foolish will perish with the senseless,
    and leave their wealth to others.

¹² Their graves are their homes forever,
  their dwelling place from age to age,
  though lands were called by their names.

¹³ In their riches, human beings do not endure;
  they are like the beasts that perish.

¹⁴ This is the way of the foolish,
  the outcome of those pleased with their lot:
¹⁵ like sheep they are driven to Sheol,
  where death shall become their shepherd,
  and the upright shall have dominion.

  Their outward show wastes away with the morning,
  and Sheol becomes their home.
¹⁶ But God will ransom my soul from the grasp of
    Sheol;
  for God indeed will receive me.

¹⁷ Then do not fear when people grow rich,
  when the glory of their houses increases.
¹⁸ They take nothing with them when they die,
  their glory does not follow them below.

¹⁹ Though they flattered themselves while they lived,
  "People will praise you for all your success,"
²⁰ yet you will go to join your forebears,
  and will never see the light anymore.

²¹ In their riches, human beings cannot discern;
  they are like the beasts that perish.

Psalm 50 (49)

¹ *A Psalm of Asaph.*

The God of gods, the LORD,
  has spoken and summoned the earth,
  from the rising of the sun to its setting.
² Out of Zion, the perfection of beauty,
  God is shining forth.

³ Our God comes, and does not keep silence.
  In advance, a fire devours,
  all around, a tempest rages,
⁴ God summons the heavens above
  and the earth, to judge the people.

⁵ "Gather my faithful ones to me,
  who made covenant with me by sacrifice."
⁶ The heavens proclaim divine righteousness,
  for God, indeed, is the judge.

⁷ "Listen, my people, I will speak;
  Israel, I will testify against you,
  for I am God, your God.

⁸ "I do not rebuke you for your sacrifices;
  your offerings are always before me.
⁹ I do not take more bullocks from your farms,
  nor goats from among your herds.

¹⁰ "For I own all the beasts of the forest,
  beasts in their thousands on my hills.
¹¹ I know all the birds on the mountains;
  all that moves in the field belongs to me.

¹² "Were I hungry, I would not tell you,
for the world and its fullness is mine.
¹³ Do I eat the flesh of bulls,
or drink the blood of goats?

¹⁴ "Give your praise as a sacrifice to God,
and fulfill your vows to the Most High.
¹⁵ Then call on me in the day of distress.
I will deliver you and you shall honor me."

¹⁶ But God will say to the wicked,
"How can you recite my commandments,
and take my covenant on your lips,
¹⁷ you who despise correction,
and cast my words behind you,

¹⁸ "You who see thieves and befriend them,
who throw in your lot with adulterers,
¹⁹ who unbridle your mouth for evil,
and yoke your tongue to deceit,

²⁰ "You who sit and malign your own kin,
and slander your own brothers and sisters?
²¹ You do this, and should I keep silence?
Do you think that I am like you?
I accuse you, lay the charge before you.

²² "Mark this, you who are forgetful of God,
lest I seize you and no one can deliver you.
²³ A sacrifice of praise gives me honor,
and to one whose way is blameless,
I will show the salvation of God."

Psalm 51 (50)

¹ For the Choirmaster. A Psalm of David ² when the prophet Nathan came to him after he had gone to Bathsheba.

³ Have mercy on me, O God,
according to your merciful love;
according to your great compassion,
blot out my transgressions.
⁴ O wash me completely from my guilt,
and cleanse me from my sin.

⁵ My transgressions, truly I know them;
my sin is always before me.
⁶ Against you, you alone, have I sinned;
what is evil in your sight I have done.
So you are just in your sentence,
without reproach in your judgment.

⁷ Behold, in guilt I was born,
a sinner when my mother conceived me.
⁸ Behold, you delight in sincerity of heart;
in secret you teach me wisdom.
⁹ Cleanse me with hyssop, and I shall be pure;
wash me, and I shall be whiter than snow.

¹⁰ Let me hear rejoicing and gladness,
that the bones you have crushed may exult.
¹¹ Turn away your face from my sins,
and blot out all my guilt.

¹² Create a pure heart for me, O God;
  renew a steadfast spirit within me.
¹³ Do not cast me away from your presence;
  take not your holy spirit from me.

¹⁴ Restore in me the joy of your salvation;
  sustain in me a willing spirit.
¹⁵ I will teach transgressors your ways,
  that sinners may return to you.

¹⁶ Rescue me from bloodshed, O God,
  O God of my salvation,
  and then my tongue shall ring out your
    righteousness.
¹⁷ O Lord, open my lips
  and my mouth shall proclaim your praise.

¹⁸ For in sacrifice you take no delight;
  burnt offering from me would not please you.
¹⁹ My sacrifice to God, a broken spirit:
  a broken and humbled heart,
  you will not spurn, O God.

²⁰ In your good pleasure, show favor to Zion;
  rebuild the walls of Jerusalem.
²¹ Then you will delight in righteous sacrifice,
  burnt offerings wholly consumed.
  Then you will be offered young bulls on your
    altar.

Psalm 52 (51)

¹ *For the Choirmaster. A* Maskil *of David* ² *after Doeg the Edomite came and told Saul, "David has gone to the house of Abimelech."*

³ Why do you boast of wickedness,
   you champion of evil?
⁴ Planning ruin all day long,
   your tongue is like a sharpened razor,
   you who practice deceit!

⁵ You love evil more than good,
   falsehood more than truth.
⁶ You love every destructive word,
   O tongue of deceit.

⁷ Then God will break you down forever,
   and will take you away,
   Will snatch you from your tent, and uproot you
   from the land of the living.

⁸ The righteous shall see and fear.
   They shall laugh and say,
⁹ "Behold the champion who refused
   to take God as a stronghold,
   but trusted in the greatness of wealth
   and grew powerful by wickedness."

¹⁰ But I am like a growing olive tree
   in the house of God.
   I trust in the faithful love of God,
   forever and ever.

¹¹ I will thank you forevermore,
   for this is your doing.
   I will hope in your name, for it is good,
   in the presence of your faithful.

Psalm 53 *(52)*

[1] *For the Choirmaster. Intoned like* Mahalat.
   A Maskil *of David.*

[2] Fools have said in their hearts,
   "There is no God."
   Their deeds are corrupt, depraved;
   no one does any good.

[3] God looks down from heaven
   on the human race,
   to see if any are wise,
   if any seek God.

[4] All have left the right path,
   depraved, every one;
   there is no one who does any good,
   no, not even one.

[5] Do none who do evil understand?
   They eat up my people as if eating bread;
   they never call out to God.

⁶ There they shall tremble with fear —
   without cause for fear —
   for God scatters the bones of your besiegers.
   They are shamed; God rejects them.

⁷ Who will bring Israel salvation from Zion?
   When God brings about the return of the people,
   then Jacob will be glad and Israel rejoice.

Psalm 54 (53)

¹ *For the Choirmaster. On stringed instruments. A*
   Maskil *of David* ² *after the Ziphites came to Saul*
   and said, "Is not David hiding among us?"

³ Save me, O God, by your name;
   by your power, defend my cause.
⁴ Hear my prayer, O God;
   give ear to the words of my mouth.

⁵ For strangers have risen against me,
   and the ruthless seek my life.
   They have no regard for God.

⁶ Behold, I have God for my help.
   The Lord sustains my soul.
⁷ Let evil recoil on my foes.
   In your faithfulness, bring them to an end.

⁸ I will sacrifice to you with willing heart,
   and praise your name, O Lord, for it is good:
⁹ for it has rescued me from all distress,
   and my eyes have gazed upon my foes.

Psalm 55 (54)

¹ *For the Choirmaster. On stringed instruments.*
    A Maskil *of David.*

² Give ear, O God, to my prayer;
    do not hide from my pleading.
³ Attend to me and reply;
    with my cares, I cannot rest.

⁴ I tremble at the shouts of the foe,
    at the cries of the wicked,
    for they pile up evil upon me;
    in anger they malign me.

⁵ My heart is stricken within me;
    death's terror falls upon me.
⁶ Trembling and fear come over me,
    and horror overwhelms me.

⁷ I say, "O that I had wings like a dove,
    to fly away and be at rest!
⁸ I would indeed escape far away,
    and take refuge in the desert.
⁹ I would hasten to find my shelter
    from the raging wind and tempest."

10 Confound and confuse their tongues, O Lord,
   for I see violence and strife in the city!
11 Night and day they patrol its walls.
   In its midst are wickedness and evil.

12 Destruction lies within it.
   Its streets are never free
   from tyranny and deceit.

13 If an enemy made taunts against me,
   I could bear it.
   If my rival had risen against me,
   I could hide from such a one.

14 But it is you, as my equal, my friend,
   whom I knew so well,
15 with whom I enjoyed friendly counsel!
   We walked together in harmony
   in the house of God.

16 May death fall suddenly upon them!
   Let them go down alive to Sheol,
   for wickedness dwells in their homes,
   and deep in their hearts.

17 As for me, I will cry to God,
   and the Lord will save me.
18 Evening, morning, and at noon,
   I will cry and lament,
   and God will hear my voice.

¹⁹ God will redeem my soul in peace
in the attack against me,
for those who fight me are many.

²⁰ God, who is enthroned forever,
will hear them and humble them.
For they will not amend their ways;
they have no fear of God.

²¹ My friend has turned against me,
has broken our pact,
²² with speech that is softer than butter,
but with a heart set on war;
with words that are smoother than oil,
but they are swords unsheathed.

²³ Entrust your cares to the LORD,
to God who will support you,
who will never allow the righteous to stumble.

²⁴ But you will bring them down, O God,
to the pit of death:
those who are deceitful and bloodthirsty
shall not live even half their days.
But I, I will trust in you, O Lord.

Psalm 56 (55)

¹ *For the Choirmaster. Intoned like "The Dove of*
    Distant Places." A Miktam *of David, when the*
    Philistines seized him in Gath.

² Have mercy on me, O God,
    for people assail me;
    they fight me all day long and oppress me.
³ My foes assail me all day long:
    many fight proudly against me.

⁴ On the day when I shall fear,
    I will trust in you,
⁵ in God, whose word I praise.
    In God I trust; I shall not fear.
    What can mere flesh do to me?

⁶ All day long they distort my words,
    their every thought against me is evil.
⁷ They band together in ambush;
    they watch my very footsteps,
    as they wait to take my life.

⁸ Repay them, O God, for their crimes;
   in your anger, bring down the peoples.
⁹ You have kept an account of my wanderings;
   you have placed my tears in your flask;
   are they not recorded in your book?

¹⁰ Then my foes will turn back
    on the day when I call to you.

   This I know, that God is on my side.
¹¹ In God, whose word I praise,
    in the LORD whose word I praise,
¹² in God I trust; I shall not fear.
    What can mere flesh do to me?

¹³ I am bound by the vows I have made you.
    O God, I will offer you praise,
¹⁴ for you have rescued my soul from death;
    you kept my feet from stumbling,
    that I may walk in the presence of God,
    in the light of the living.

Psalm 57 (56)

¹ *For the Choirmaster. Intoned like "Do not destroy."*
A Miktam of David when he fled from Saul into
a cave.

² Have mercy on me, God, have mercy,
for in you my soul has taken refuge.
In the shadow of your wings I take refuge,
till the storms of destruction pass by.

³ I call to you, God the Most High,
to God who provides for me.
⁴ O send from heaven and save me,
and put to shame those who assail me.
O send your loving mercy and faithfulness.

⁵ My soul lies down among lions,
who would devour human prey.
Their teeth are spears and arrows,
their tongue a sharpened sword.
⁶ Be exalted, O God, above the heavens,
your glory over all the earth!

⁷ They laid down a net for my steps;
   my soul was bowed down.
   They dug a pit in my path,
   but fell in it themselves.

⁸ My heart is ready, O God;
   my heart is ready.
   I will sing, I will sing your praise.
⁹ Awake, my soul!
   Awake, O lyre and harp!
   I will awake the dawn.

¹⁰ I will praise you, Lord, among the peoples,
   among the nations sing psalms to you,
¹¹ for your mercy reaches to the heavens,
   and your truth to the skies.
¹² Be exalted, O God, above the heavens;
   may your glory shine on all the earth!

Psalm 58 *(57)*

¹ *For the Choirmaster. Intoned like "Do not destroy."*
   A Miktam *of David.*

² Do you truly decree the right,
   you who hold divine power?
   Do you judge rightly the human race?
³ No, in your hearts you devise iniquities;
   your hands deal out violence to the land.

⁴ The wicked go astray from the womb;
   deviant from birth, they speak lies.
⁵ Their venom is like the venom of the snake;
   they are like a deaf viper stopping its ears,
⁶ lest it should hear the snake-charmer's voice,
   the voice of the skillful dealer in spells.

⁷ O God, break the teeth in their mouths;
   tear out the fangs of these lions, O Lord!
⁸ Let them vanish like water that runs away;
   let them wither like grass that is trodden
            underfoot.
⁹ Let them be like the snail that dissolves into slime,
   like a woman's miscarriage that never sees the sun.

¹⁰ Before they put forth thorns, like a bramble,
   let them be swept away, green wood or dry!
¹¹ The righteous shall rejoice at the sight of
         vengeance;
   they shall bathe their feet in the blood of the
         wicked.
¹² People shall say: "Truly, the righteous are
         rewarded.
   Truly there is a God who judges on earth."

Psalm 59 (58)

¹ *For the Choirmaster. Intoned like "Do not destroy."*
   A Miktam *of David when Saul sent men to keep*
   watch on his house and kill him.

² Rescue me, God, from my foes;
   protect me from those who attack me.
³ O rescue me from those who do evil,
   and save me from those who are bloodthirsty.

⁴ See, they lie in wait for my life;
   the strong band together against me.
   For no offense, no sin of mine, O LORD,
⁵ for no guilt of mine they rush to take their stand.

   Awake! Come to meet me, and see!
⁶ LORD God of hosts, you are Israel's God.
   Rouse yourself and punish the nations;
   show no mercy to evil traitors.
⁷ Each evening they come back;
   howling like dogs, they roam about the city.

⁸ See how their mouths utter insults;
   their lips are like sharpened swords.
   "For who," they say, "will hear us?"
⁹ But you, LORD, will laugh them to scorn.
   You make a mockery of all the nations.

¹⁰ O my Strength, for you will I watch,
   for you, O God, are my stronghold,
¹¹ the God who shows me faithful love.

Now God will proceed before me,
God will let me look upon my foes.
¹² Do not kill them lest my people forget;
rout them by your power, lay them low.

It is you, O Lord, who are our shield.
¹³ For the sins of their mouths and the words of
   their lips,
let them be caught in their pride;
for the curses and lies that they speak.

¹⁴ Consume them, consume them in anger
till they are no more.
Then they will know that God is the ruler
over Jacob and the ends of the earth.

¹⁵ Each evening they come back;
they howl like dogs and roam about the city.
¹⁶ They prowl in search of food;
they growl till they have their fill.

¹⁷ As for me, I will sing of your strength,
and acclaim your faithful love in the morning,
for you have been my stronghold,
a refuge in the day of my distress.

¹⁸ O my Strength, to you I will sing praise,
for you, O God, are my stronghold,
the God who shows me faithful love.

Psalm 60 (59)

¹ *For the Choirmaster. Intoned like "The Lily of*
   Testimony." A Miktam *of David for instruction*
   when he went out against the Aram-Haharaim
   and Aram-Sobah, and when Joab returned to
   Edom and defeated twelve thousand in the Valley
   of Salt.

³ O God, you have rejected us, and broken us.
   You have been angry; come back to us.

⁴ You have made the earth quake, torn it open.
   Repair what is shattered, for it sways.
⁵ You have inflicted hardships on your people,
   made us drink a wine that dazed us.

⁶ For those who fear you, you gave the signal
   to flee from the face of the bow.
⁷ With your right hand, grant salvation, and give
      answer,
   that those whom you love may be free.

⁸ From the sanctuary God has spoken:
   "I will exult, and divide the land of Shechem;
   I will measure out the valley of Succoth.

[9] "Mine is Gilead, mine is Manasseh;
  Ephraim I take for my helmet,
  Judah is my scepter.

[10] "Moab is my washbowl;
  on Edom I will cast my shoe.
  Over Philistia I will shout in triumph."

[11] But who will lead me to the fortified city?
  Who will bring me to Edom?
[12] Have you, O God, rejected us?
  Will you march with our armies no longer?

[13] Give us aid against the foe,
  for human help is vain.
[14] With God we shall do bravely,
  and God will trample down our foes.

Psalm 61 (60)

¹ *For the Choirmaster. With stringed instruments. Of David.*

² Listen, O God, to my cry!
   Attend to my prayer!
³ From the end of the earth I call you;
   my heart is faint.

   Set me high upon the rock
   too high for me to reach,
⁴ you, my refuge and mighty tower
   against the foe.

⁵ Then will I dwell in your tent forever,
   and hide in the shelter of your wings.
⁶ For you, O God, have heard my vows;
   you have given me the heritage
   of those who fear your name.

⁷ Day upon day you will add to the king;
   his years as age upon age.
⁸ May he ever sit enthroned before God:
   bid mercy and truth be his protection.
⁹ So I will sing to your name forever,
   and day after day fulfill my vows.

Psalm 62 *(61)*

¹ *For the Choirmaster. Intoned like Jeduthun. A Psalm of David.*

² In God alone is my soul at rest,
   my salvation comes from the Lord.
³ God alone is my rock, my salvation,
   my fortress; I shall not greatly falter.

⁴ How long will you attack one alone,
   break down your victim,
   as you would a tottering wall,
   or a tumbling fence?

⁵ Their plan is only to bring down someone of
      prominence;
   they take pleasure in lies.
   With their mouth they utter blessing,
   but in their heart they curse.

⁶ Be at rest, my soul, in God alone,
   from whom comes my hope.
⁷ God alone is my rock, my salvation,
   my fortress; I shall not falter.

⁸ In God is my salvation and my glory,
   my rock of strength;
   in God is my refuge.
⁹ Trust at all times, O people;
   pour out your hearts to God, our refuge.

¹⁰ The children of Adam are a breath,
    an illusion, people of rank.
    Placed on the scales, they rise;
    they all weigh less than a breath.

¹¹ Do not put your trust in oppression,
    nor vain hopes on plunder.
    Even if riches increase,
    set not your heart on them.

¹² For God has said only one thing;
    only two have I heard:
    that to God alone belongs power,
¹³ and to you, Lord, faithful love;
    and that you repay each of us
    according to our deeds.

Psalm 63 (62)

¹ *A Psalm of David when he was in the desert of Judah.*

² O God, you are my God; at dawn I seek you;
  for you my soul is thirsting.
  For you my flesh is pining,
  like a dry, weary land without water.
³ I have come before you in the holy place,
  to behold your strength and your glory.

⁴ Your faithful love is better than life;
  my lips will speak your praise.
⁵ I will bless you all my life;
  in your name I will lift up my hands.
⁶ My soul shall be filled as with a banquet;
  with joyful lips, my mouth shall praise you.

⁷ When I remember you upon my bed,
  I muse on you through the watches of the night.
⁸ For you have been my strength;
  in the shadow of your wings I rejoice.
⁹ My soul clings fast to you;
  your right hand upholds me.

¹⁰ Those who seek to destroy my life
    shall go down to the depths of the earth.
¹¹ Put to the power of the sword,
    they shall be left as prey for the jackals.

¹² But the king shall rejoice in God;
    all that swear by the Lord shall exult,
    for the mouth of liars shall be silenced.

Psalm 64 (63)

¹ For the Choirmaster. A Psalm of David.

² Hear, O God, the voice of my complaint;
   guard my life from dread of the foe.
³ From the assembly of the wicked, hide me,
   from the throng of those who do evil.

⁴ They sharpen their tongues like swords.
   They aim bitter words like arrows,
⁵ to shoot at the innocent from ambush,
   shooting suddenly and fearlessly.

⁶ Holding firm in their evil course,
   they conspire to lay secret snares.
   They are saying, "Who will see us?
⁷ Who can search out our crimes?"

   They have hatched their wicked plots,
   and brought their plots to perfection.
   How profound the depths of the heart!

8 God will shoot them with arrows,
   and deal them sudden wounds.
9 Their own tongue will bring them to ruin;
   all who see them will shake their heads.

10 Then will all be afraid;
    they will tell what God has done.
    They will ponder God's deeds.
11 The righteous will rejoice in the LORD,
    in whom they shall take refuge.
    All upright hearts will glory.

Psalm 65 (64)

For the Choirmaster. A Psalm of David. A Song.

2 Praise is due to you in Zion, O God.
  To you we pay our vows in Jerusalem,
3 you who hear our prayer.
  To you all flesh will come.
4 Our evil deeds are too heavy for us,
  but only you can pardon our transgressions.

5 Blessed the one whom you choose and call
  to dwell in your courts.
  We are filled with the good things of your house,
  of your holy temple.

6 With wondrous deliverance you answer us,
  O God our savior.
  You are the hope of all the earth,
  and of far distant seas.

7 You establish the mountains with your strength;
  you are girded with power.
8 You still the roaring of the seas,
  the roaring of their waves,
  and the tumult of the peoples.

⁹ Distant peoples stand in awe
   at your wondrous deeds.
   The lands of sunrise and sunset
   you fill with your joy.

¹⁰ You visit the earth, give it water;
   you fill it with riches.
   God's ever-flowing river brims over
   to prepare the grain.

   And thus it is you who prepare it:
¹¹ you drench its furrows;
   you level it, soften it with showers;
   you bless its growth.

¹² You crown the year with your bounty,
   and abundance flows in your pathways.
¹³ The pastures of the desert overflow,
   and the hills are girded with joy,

¹⁴ The meadows are clothed with flocks,
   and the valleys are decked with wheat.
   They shout for joy, and even sing!

Psalm 66 (65)

¹ *For the Choirmaster. A Song. A Psalm.*

Cry out with joy to God, all the earth;
² O sing to the glory of God's name.
O render glorious praise.
³ Say to God, "How awesome your deeds!

Because of the greatness of your strength,
your enemies cower before you.
⁴ Before you all the earth shall bow down,
shall sing to you, sing to your name!"

⁵ Come and see the works of God:
awesome deeds among the children of Adam.
⁶ God turned the sea into dry land;
they passed through the river on foot.

There did we rejoice in the Lord,
⁷ who rules forever with might,
whose eyes keep watch on the nations:
let rebels not exalt themselves.

⁸ O peoples, bless our God;
let our voice of praise resound,
⁹ to the God who gave life to our souls
and kept our feet from stumbling.

¹⁰ For you, O God, have tested us,
    you have tried us as silver is tried;
¹¹ you led us, God, into the snare;
    you laid a heavy burden on our backs.

¹² You let people ride over our heads;
    we went through fire and through water,
    but then you brought us to a place of plenty.

¹³ Burnt offering I bring to your house;
    to you I will pay my vows,
¹⁴ the vows which my lips have uttered,
    which my mouth declared in my distress.

¹⁵ I will offer you burnt offerings of fatlings
    with the smoke of sacrificial rams.
    I will offer bullocks and goats.

¹⁶ Come and hear, all who fear God;
    I will tell what God has done for my soul.
¹⁷ To the Lord I cried aloud,
    with exaltation ready on my tongue.

¹⁸ Had I cherished evil in my heart,
    the Lord would not have listened.
¹⁹ But truly God has listened,
    and has heeded the voice of my prayer.
²⁰ Blest be God, who did not reject my prayer,
    nor withhold from me faithful love.

Psalm 67 (66)

¹ For the Choirmaster. With string instruments.
A Psalm. A Song.

² May God be gracious and bless us.
Let your face shed its light upon us.
³ So will your ways be known upon earth
and all nations learn your salvation.

⁴ Let the peoples praise you, O God;
let all the peoples praise you.

⁵ Let the nations be glad and shout for joy,
with uprightness you rule the peoples;
you guide the nations on earth.

⁶ Let the peoples praise you, O God;
let all the peoples praise you.

⁷ The earth has yielded its fruit
for God, our God, has blessed us.
⁸ May God still give us his blessing,
and be revered to all the ends of the earth.

Psalm 68 (67)

¹ *For the Choirmaster. Of David. A Psalm. A Song.*

² Let God arise; let all foes be scattered.
  Let those who hate the Lord flee from the presence.
³ As smoke is driven away, so drive them away;
  like wax that melts before the fire,
    so the wicked shall perish at the presence of God.

⁴ But the righteous shall rejoice at the presence of
    God;
  they shall exult with glad rejoicing.
⁵ O sing to God; make music to God's name.
  Extol the One who rides on the clouds,
    whose name is the Lᴏʀᴅ, in whose presence we
      exult.

⁶ Father of orphans, defender of widows:
  such is God in the holy place.
⁷ God gives the desolate a home to dwell in,
  and leads the prisoners forth into prosperity,
  while rebels must dwell in a parched land.

⁸ O God, when you went forth before your people,
  when you marched across the desert,
⁹ the earth trembled, heavens poured down rain
  at the presence of God, the God of Sinai,
  at the presence of God, the God of Israel.

¹⁰ You poured down, O God, a generous rain;
   when your heritage languished, you restored it.
¹¹ It was there that your flock began to dwell.
   In your goodness, O God, you provided for the
        poor.

¹² The Lord announces the command;
   a mighty throng of maidens bears good tidings:
¹³ "Kings with their armies will flee, will flee,
   and at home the women already share the spoil,
¹⁴ though they are at rest among the sheepfolds:

   They are covered with silver as the wings of a
        dove,
   its feathers brilliant with shining gold.
¹⁵ When the Almighty scatters kings on the
        mountain,
   it is like snow that whitens Mount Zalmon."

¹⁶ O godly mountain, mountain of Bashan;
   O many-peaked mountain, mountain of Bashan!
¹⁷ Why look with envy, you many-peaked
        mountain,
   at the mountain where God has desired to dwell?
   It is there that the LORD shall dwell forever.

¹⁸ The chariots of God are thousands upon thousands.
　The Lord has come from Sinai to the holy place.
¹⁹ You have ascended on high, leading captivity
　　　captive;
　receiving people as tribute,
　so that even the rebellious may dwell near the
　　　LORD God.

²⁰ Day after day, may the Lord be blest
　who bears our burdens; God is our savior.
²¹ This God of ours is a God who saves.
　The LORD our Lord provides an escape from death.
²² And God will smite the heads of foes,
　the hairy crown of those who walk about in guilt.

²³ The Lord said, "I will bring them back from
　　　Bashan;
　I will bring them back from the depth of the sea.
²⁴ Then you will bathe your feet in their blood,
　and the tongues of your dogs take their share of
　　　the foe."

²⁵ They see your solemn procession, O God,
　the procession of my God, of my king, to the holy
　　　place:
²⁶ the singers in the forefront, the musicians coming
　　　last;
　between them, maidens sounding their timbrels.

²⁷ "In the sacred assembly, bless God, the LORD,
O you, from the fountain of Israel."
²⁸ There is Benjamin, least of the tribes, at the head;
Judah's princes, a mighty throng;
Zebulun's princes, Naphtali's princes.

²⁹ Summon forth your might, O God;
your might, O God, which you have shown for us.
³⁰ From your temple high in Jerusalem,
kings will come to you bringing their tribute.

³¹ Rebuke the wild beast that dwells in the reeds,
the herd of bulls among the calves of the peoples:
They prostrate themselves with plates of silver.
Scatter the nations who delight in wars.
³² Rich merchants will make their way from Egypt;
Ethiopia will stretch out her hands to God.

³³ You kingdoms of the earth, sing to God, praise
the Lord
³⁴ who rides on the heavens, the ancient heavens.
Behold, the Lord thunders with a mighty voice.

³⁵ Come, let us acknowledge the power of God,
whose glory is on Israel; whose might is in the
skies.
³⁶ Awesome are you, O God, in your holy place,
You who are the God of Israel.
You give strength and power to your people.
Blest be God!

Psalm 69 *(68)*

1 *For the Choirmaster. Intoned like "Lilies."*
   Of David.

2 Save me, O God, for the waters
   have risen to my neck.
3 I have sunk into the mud of the deep,
   where there is no foothold.
   I have entered the waters of the deep,
   where the flood overwhelms me.

4 I am wearied with crying aloud;
   my throat is parched.
   My eyes are wasted away
   with waiting for my God.

5 More numerous than the hairs on my head
   are those who hate me without cause.
   Mighty are those who attack me,
   enemies with lies.
   What I have never stolen,
   how can I restore?

6 O God, you know my folly;
   from you my sins are not hidden.
7 May those who hope in you not be shamed
   because of me, O Lord of hosts;
   may those who seek you not be disgraced
   because of me, O God of Israel.

8 It is for you that I suffer taunts,
   that shame has covered my face.
9 To my own kin I have become an outcast,
   a stranger to the children of my mother.
10 Zeal for your house consumes me,
   and taunts against you fall on me.

11 When my soul wept bitterly in fasting,
   they made it a taunt against me.
12 When I made my clothing sackcloth,
   I became a reproach to them,
13 the gossip of those at the gates,
   the theme of drunkards' songs.

14 But I pray to you, O Lord,
   at an acceptable time.
   In your great mercy, answer me, O God,
   with your faithful salvation.

15 Rescue me from the mire, lest I sink.
   From those who hate me, deliver me,
   and from the waters of the deep,
16 lest the waves overwhelm me.
   Let not the deep engulf me,
   nor the pit close its mouth on me.

¹⁷ LORD, answer, for your love is kind;
    in your abundant compassion, turn towards me.
¹⁸ Do not hide your face from your servant;
    answer me quickly, for I am in distress.
¹⁹ Come close to my soul and redeem me;
    ransom me because of my foes.

²⁰ You know my taunts, my shame, my dishonor;
    my oppressors are all before you.
²¹ Taunts have broken my heart;
    here I am in anguish.
    I looked for solace, but there was none;
    for consolers—not one could I find.

²² For food they gave me gall;
    in my thirst they gave me vinegar to drink.
²³ Let their table be a snare to them,
    and for their friends, a trap.
²⁴ Let their eyes grow dim and blind;
    let their limbs continually tremble.

²⁵ Pour out your anger upon them;
    let your burning fury overtake them.
²⁶ Let their camp be left desolate;
    let no one dwell in their tents:
²⁷ for they persecute one whom you struck;
    they increase the pain of one whom you
      wounded.

²⁸ Charge them with guilt upon guilt;
   let them have no share in your justice.
²⁹ Blot them out from the book of the living;
   do not enroll them among the righteous.

³⁰ As for me in my poverty and pain,
   let your salvation, O God, raise me up.
³¹ Then I will praise God's name with a song;
   I will glorify the Lord with thanksgiving:
³² a gift pleasing the LORD more than oxen,
   more than a bull with horns and hooves.

³³ The poor when they see it will be glad,
   and God-seeking hearts will revive;
³⁴ for the LORD attends the needy,
   and does not spurn those in their chains.
³⁵ Let the heavens and the earth give praise to God,
   the seas and everything that moves in them.

³⁶ For God will bring salvation to Zion,
   and rebuild the cities of Judah,
   and they shall dwell there in possession.
³⁷ The children of God's servants shall inherit it;
   those who love the Lord's name shall dwell there.

Psalm 70 (69)

¹ *For the Choirmaster. Of David. A Memorial.*

² O God, come to my assistance;
   O Lord, make haste to help me!
³ Let there be shame and confusion
   on those who seek my life.

   O let them turn back in confusion,
   who delight in my harm;
⁴ let them turn because of their shame,
   who jeer at me and mock.

⁵ O let there be rejoicing and gladness
   for all who seek you.
   Let them say forever, "God is great,"
   who love your saving help.

⁶ As for me, who am wretched and poor,
   hasten to me, O God.
   You are my rescuer, my help;
   O Lord, do not delay.

Psalm 71 (70)

[1] In you, O LORD, I take refuge;
  let me never be put to shame.
[2] In your righteousness, rescue me, free me;
  incline your ear to me and save me.

[3] Be my rock, my constant refuge,
  a mighty stronghold to save me,
  for you are my rock, my stronghold.
[4] My God, free me from the hand of the wicked,
  from the grip of the unjust, of the oppressor.

[5] It is you, O Lord, who are my hope,
  my trust, O LORD, from my youth.
[6] On you I have leaned from my birth;
  it was you who took me from my mother's womb.
  At all times I give you praise.

[7] My fate has filled many with awe,
  but you are my mighty refuge.
[8] My mouth is filled with your praise,
  with your glory, all the day long.
[9] Do not reject me now that I am old;
  when my strength fails do not forsake me.

¹⁰ For my enemies are speaking about me;
 those who watch me take counsel together.
¹¹ They say God has forsaken me;
 they can seize me, for no one will save me.
¹² O God, do not stay far off;
 O my God, make haste to help me!

¹³ Let them be put to shame and consumed,
 those who seek my life.
 Let them be covered with shame and confusion,
 those who seek to harm me.

¹⁴ But as for me, I will always hope,
 and praise you more and more.
¹⁵ My mouth will tell of your righteousness,
 and all the day long of your salvation,
 though I can never tell it all.

¹⁶ I will come with praise of your might, O Lord;
 I will call to mind your righteousness,
 yours, O Lord, alone.

¹⁷ O God, you have taught me from my youth,
 and I proclaim your wonders still.
¹⁸ Even till I am old and gray-headed,
 do not forsake me, O God.

Let me tell of your mighty arm
to every coming generation;
¹⁹ your strength and your justice, O God,
reach to the highest heavens.
It is you who have worked such wonders.
O God, who is like you?

²⁰ You have made me witness many troubles and
evils,
but you will give me back my life.
You will raise me from the depths of the earth;
²¹ you will exalt me and console me again.

²² So I will give you thanks on the lyre
for your faithfulness, O my God.
To you will I sing with the harp,
to you, the Holy One of Israel.
²³ When I sing to you, my lips shall shout for joy,
and my soul, which you have redeemed.

²⁴ And all the day long my tongue
shall tell the tale of your righteousness,
for they are put to shame and disgraced,
those who sought to harm me.

Psalm 72 (71)

[1] *Of Solomon.*

O God, give your judgment to the king,
to a king's son your righteousness,
[2] that he may judge your people in righteousness,
and your poor in right judgment.

[3] May the mountains bring forth peace for the
people,
and the hills bear peace in righteousness.
[4] May he defend the poor of the people,
and save the children of the needy,
and crush the oppressor.

[5] He shall endure like the sun and the moon
through all generations.
[6] He shall descend like rain on the meadow,
like showers that water the earth.
[7] In his days shall righteousness flourish,
and great peace till the moon is no more.

[8] He shall rule from sea to sea,
from the River to the bounds of the earth.
[9] Let the desert dwellers fall before him,
and his enemies lick the dust.

¹⁰ The kings of Tarshish and the islands
    shall pay him tribute.
    The kings of Sheba and Seba
    shall bring him gifts.
¹¹ Before him all kings shall fall prostrate,
    all nations shall serve him.

¹² For he shall rescue the needy when they cry,
    the poor who have no one to help.
¹³ He will have pity on the weak and the needy,
    and save the lives of the needy.
¹⁴ From oppression and violence he redeems their
       life;
    to him their blood is dear.

¹⁵ Long may he live, and the gold of Sheba be given
       him.
    They shall pray for him without ceasing,
    and bless him all the day.

¹⁶ May grain be abundant in the land,
    waving to the peaks of the mountains.
    May its fruit rustle like Lebanon;
    may the people flourish in the cities
    like grass on the earth.

¹⁷ May his name endure forever,
   his name continue like the sun.
   Every tribe shall be blest in him,
   all nations shall call him blessed.

*   *   *

[18] Blest be the LORD, God of Israel,
   who alone works wonders,
[19] Ever blest the glorious name of the Lord.
   Let the glory of God fill the earth.
   Amen! Amen!

[20] Here end the Psalms of David, son of Jesse.

BOOK THREE
OF THE PSALTER

Psalm 73 (72)

¹ *A Psalm of Asaph.*

How good is God to Israel,
to those who are pure of heart!
² As for me, my feet came close to stumbling;
my steps had almost slipped,
³ for I was filled with envy of the proud,
when I saw how the wicked prosper.

⁴ For them there are no pains;
their bodies are sound and sleek.
⁵ They do not share in people's burdens;
they are not stricken like others.

⁶ So they wear their pride like a necklace;
they clothe themselves with violence.
⁷ With folds of fat, their eyes protrude.
With imagination their hearts overflow.

⁸ They scoff; they speak with malice.
From on high they threaten oppression.
⁹ They have set their mouths in the heavens,
and their tongues are roaming the earth.

¹⁰ So the people turn to them
    and drink in all their words.
¹¹ Thus they say, "How can God know?
    Does the Most High have any knowledge?"
¹² Look at them, such are the wicked;
    ever prosperous, they grow in wealth.

¹³ How useless to keep my heart pure,
    and wash my hands in innocence,
¹⁴ when I was stricken all day long,
    suffered punishment with each new morning.
¹⁵ Then I said, "If I should speak like that,
    I should betray the race of your children."

¹⁶ I strove to fathom this problem,
    too hard for my mind to understand,
¹⁷ until I entered the holy place of God,
    and came to discern their end.

¹⁸ How slippery the paths on which you set them;
    you make them fall to destruction.
¹⁹ How suddenly they come to their ruin,
    swept away, destroyed by terrors.
²⁰ Like a dream one wakes from, O Lord,
    when you wake you dismiss them as phantoms.

²¹ And so when my heart grew embittered,
and I was pierced to the depths of my being,
²² I was stupid and did not understand;
I was like a beast in your sight.

²³ As for me, I was always in your presence;
you were holding me by my right hand.
²⁴ By your counsel you will guide me,
and then you will lead me to glory.

²⁵ What else have I in heaven but you?
Apart from you, I want nothing on earth.
²⁶ My flesh and my heart waste away;
God is the strength of my heart,
my portion forever.

²⁷ Surely, those who are far from you perish;
you put an end to all those who are unfaithful.
²⁸ For me to be near God is good;
I have made the Lord GOD my refuge.
I will proclaim your works
at the gates of daughter Zion.

Psalm 74 (73)

[1] *A Maskil of Asaph.*

Why, O God, have you cast us off forever?
Why does your anger blaze at the sheep of your
pasture?
[2] Remember your flock which you claimed long
ago,
the tribe you redeemed to be your own possession,
this mountain of Zion where you made your
dwelling.

[3] Turn your steps to these places that are utterly
ruined!
The enemy has laid waste the whole of the holy
place.
[4] Your foes have made uproar in the midst of your
assembly;
they have set up their emblems as tokens there.
[5] They have wielded their axes on high,
as at the entrance to a grove of trees.

[6] They have broken down all the carvings;
they have struck together with hatchet and
pickaxe.
[7] They have set your holy place on fire;
they have razed and profaned the abode of your
name.

⁸ They said in their hearts, "We will utterly crush
    them;
  we will burn every shrine of God in the land."
⁹ We do not see our emblems, nor is there a
    prophet;
  we have no one to tell us how long it will last.

¹⁰ How long, O God, is the enemy to scoff?
   Is the foe to insult your name forever?
¹¹ Why do you hold back your hand?
   Why do you keep your right hand hidden in
     your cloak?

¹² Yet it is God who reigns from of old,
   who bestows salvation through all the land.
¹³ It was you who divided the sea by your might,
   who shattered the heads of the monsters in the
     sea.

¹⁴ It was you who crushed Leviathan's heads,
   and gave it as food to the beasts of the desert.
¹⁵ It was you who opened up springs and torrents;
   it was you who dried up ever-flowing rivers.

¹⁶ Yours is the day and yours is the night;
   it was you who established the light and the sun.
¹⁷ It was you who fixed the bounds of the earth,
   you who made both summer and winter.

[18] Remember this, O Lord: the enemy scoffed!
A senseless people insulted your name!
[19] Do not give the soul of your dove to the beasts,
nor forget the life of your poor ones forever.

[20] Look to the covenant; for caves in the land
are places where violence makes its home.
[21] Do not let the oppressed be put to shame;
let the poor and the needy bless your name.

[22] Arise, O God, and defend your cause!
Remember how the senseless revile you all the
day.
[23] Do not forget the clamor of your foes,
the unceasing uproar of those who defy you.

Psalm 75 *(74)*

[1] *For the Choirmaster. Intoned like "Do not destroy."
A Psalm of Asaph. A Song.*

[2] We give praise to you, O God;
we give praise, for your name is near.
We recount your wonderful deeds.

³ "When I establish the appointed time,
   then I myself will judge with fairness.
⁴ Though the earth and all who dwell in it may
      rock,
   it is I who set firm its pillars.

⁵ To the boastful I say, 'Do not boast';
   to the wicked, 'Do not flaunt your strength,
⁶ do not exalt your strength on high.
   Do not speak with insolent pride.'"

⁷ For neither from the east nor from the west,
   nor from the desert comes exaltation.
⁸ For God alone is the judge,
   who humbles one and exalts another.

⁹ For in the hand of the LORD is a cup,
   full of wine, both foaming and spiced.
   God pours it; they drain it to the dregs;
   all the wicked on the earth must drain it.
¹⁰ As for me, I will rejoice forever,
   and sing psalms to the God of Jacob.

¹¹ I shall break the strength of the wicked,
   while the strength of the just will be exalted.

Psalm 76 (75)

1 *For the Choirmaster. With String Instruments.*
   A Psalm of Asaph. A Song.

2 O God, you are renowned in Judah;
   in Israel your name is great.
3 You set up your tent in Salem,
   and your dwelling place in Zion.
4 It was there you broke the flaming arrows,
   the shield, the sword, the armor.

5 Resplendent are you, more majestic
   than the everlasting mountains.
6 The stouthearted, despoiled, sank into slumber;
   none of the soldiers could lift a hand.
7 At your threat, O God of Jacob,
   horse and rider lay stunned.

8 You, you alone, strike terror.
   Who can stand in your presence,
   against the might of your wrath?

⁹ You uttered your sentence from the heavens;
the earth in terror was still

¹⁰ when you arose, O God, to judge,
to save all the humble of the earth.

¹¹ For human rage only serves to praise you;
you surround yourself with the survivors of
wrath.

¹² Make vows to the LORD your God and fulfill
them.
Let all around pay tribute to the One who strikes
terror,

¹³ who cuts short the breath of leaders,
who strikes terror in the rulers of the earth.

Psalm 77 (76)

¹ *For the Choirmaster. Intoned like "Jeduthun."*
   Of Asaph. A Psalm.

² I cry aloud to God,
   cry aloud to God that I be heard.

³ In the day of my distress I seek the Lord.
   In the night my hands are raised unwearied;
   my soul refuses comfort.
⁴ As I remember my God, I groan.
   I ponder, and my spirit faints.

⁵ You keep my eyes from closing.
   I am troubled, unable to speak.
⁶ I think of the days of long ago,
   and remember the years long past.
⁷ At night I muse within my heart.
   I ponder, and my spirit questions.

⁸ "Will the Lord reject us forever,
   and show divine favor no more?
⁹ Has God's faithful kindness vanished forever?
   Has the promise come to an end,
¹⁰ or God's mercy been forgotten,
   or compassion withdrawn in anger?"

¹¹ I said, "This is what causes my grief:
that the right hand of the Most High has changed."
¹² I remember the deeds of the LORD,
I remember your wonders of old;
¹³ I muse on all your works,
and ponder your mighty deeds.

¹⁴ Your way, O God, is holy.
What god is as great as our God?
¹⁵ You are the God who works wonders.
Among the peoples you showed your power.
¹⁶ Your strong arm redeemed your people,
the descendants of Jacob and Joseph.

¹⁷ The waters saw you, O God;
the waters saw you and anguished.
Yes, the depths were moved to tremble.
¹⁸ The clouds poured down with rain.
The skies sent forth their voice;
your arrows flashed to and fro.

¹⁹ Your thunderous voice was in the whirlwind;
your flashes lighted up the world.
The earth was moved and trembled.
²⁰ Your way was through the sea,
your path through the mighty waters,
but the trace of your steps was not seen.

²¹ You guided your people like a flock
by the hand of Moses and Aaron.

Psalm 78 *(77)*

¹ *A Maskil of Asaph.*

Give ear, my people, to my teaching;
  incline your ear to the words of my mouth.
² I will open my mouth in a parable
  and utter hidden lessons of the past.

³ The things we have heard and understood,
  the things our parents have told us,
⁴ these we will not hide from our children
  but will tell them to the next generation:
  the glories and the might of the Lord,
  and the marvelous deeds that have been done.

⁵ God established a decree in Jacob,
  and set up a law in Israel.
  Our forebears were given a command
  to make it known to their children,
⁶ that the next generation might know it,
  the children yet to be born.

They should arise and declare it to their children,
⁷ that they should set their hope in God,
  and never forget God's deeds,
  but keep every one of the commandments,

⁸ So that they might not be like their forebears,
a defiant and rebellious generation,
a generation whose heart was fickle,
whose spirit was not faithful to God.

⁹ The Ephraimites, armed with the bow,
turned back on the day of battle.
¹⁰ They failed to keep God's covenant,
refused to walk according to the law.

¹¹ They forgot the things God had done,
the wondrous works that had been shown them,
¹² wonders worked in the sight of their forebears,
in Egypt, in the plains of Zoan.

¹³ God divided the sea and led them through,
and made the waters stand up like a wall.
¹⁴ By day the Lord led them with a cloud;
throughout the night, with a light of fire.

¹⁵ The Lord split the rocks in the desert,
gave them plentiful drink, as from the deep,
¹⁶ making streams flow out from the rock,
and waters flow down like rivers.

¹⁷ Yet still they sinned against God,
rebelled against the Most High in the desert.
¹⁸ In their heart they put God to the test
by demanding the food they craved.

¹⁹ They spoke against God and said:
   "Can God spread a table in the wilderness?
²⁰ Behold, it was the Lord who struck the rock:
   water gushed forth and swept down in torrents.
   But can the Most High give us bread?
   Can God provide meat for the people?"

²¹ Upon hearing this, the LORD was angry.
   A fire was kindled against Jacob;
   divine anger rose against Israel.
²² For they had no faith in God,
   did not trust the saving power of the Lord.

²³ Yet God commanded the clouds above,
   and opened the gates of heaven,
²⁴ rained down manna for them to eat,
   and gave them bread from heaven.

²⁵ Human beings ate the bread of angels;
   the Lord sent them an abundance of food,
²⁶ stirring up the east wind in the heavens,
   and directing the south wind with might.

²⁷ The Lord rained flesh upon them like dust,
   winged fowl like the sands of the sea,
²⁸ letting it fall in the midst of their camp,
   and all around their tents.

²⁹ So they ate and had their fill,
  what they craved, God gave them.

³⁰ But before they had sated their hunger,
  while the food was still in their mouths,
³¹ God rose in anger against them
  and slew the strongest among them,
  struck down the flower of Israel.

³² Despite all this, they kept on sinning;
  they failed to believe divine wonders.
³³ So God ended their days like a breath,
  and their years in sudden terror.

³⁴ When they were slain, then they sought the
      Lord;
  repented and earnestly sought God.
³⁵ They would remember that God was their rock,
  God the Most High their redeemer.

³⁶ Yet they deceived the Lord with their mouths;
  they lied with their tongues.
³⁷ For their hearts were not steadfast toward God;
  they were not faithful to the covenant.

³⁸ Yet God who is full of compassion
  forgave them their sin and spared them,
  so often held back divine anger,
  and did not stir up all godly rage.
³⁹ God remembered they were only flesh,
  a breath that passes, never to return.

⁴⁰ They rebelled against God often in the desert,
  and caused the Lord pain in the wasteland!
⁴¹ Yet again they turned and tested God;
  they provoked the Holy One of Israel.

⁴² They failed to remember God's deeds
  on the day they were redeemed from the foe,
⁴³ when signs were performed in Egypt,
  and wonders in the plains of Zoan.

⁴⁴ The Lord turned their rivers into blood;
  they could not drink from their streams.
⁴⁵ God sent swarms of flies to devour them,
  and frogs to destroy them;
⁴⁶ gave their crops to insects,
  the fruit of their labor to the locust.

⁴⁷ The Lord destroyed their vines with hail,
  their sycamore trees with frost;
⁴⁸ gave up their cattle to hail,
  their herds to darts of lightning.

⁴⁹ God unleashed on them the heat of heaven's
       anger,
   fury, rage and havoc,
   a troop of destroying angels.

⁵⁰ God leveled a path for his anger,
   and did not spare their lives from death,
   but gave their livestock to the plague.
⁵¹ The Lord struck all the firstborn in Egypt,
   the first vigor of youth from the dwellings of Ham.

⁵² Then God brought forth the people like sheep,
   led them like a flock in the desert,
⁵³ led them safely with nothing to fear,
   while the sea engulfed their foes.

⁵⁴ So the Lord brought them to the holy land,
   to the mountain won by God's right hand,
⁵⁵ driving out the nations before them,
   and apportioning to each their heritage.
   The tribes of Israel were settled in their tents.

⁵⁶ With defiance they tested God Most High;
   they refused to obey divine decrees.
⁵⁷ They strayed as faithless as their forebears;
   like a treacherous bow, betrayed the Lord.
⁵⁸ With their high places they provoked God to
       wrath,
   to jealousy by serving their idols.

⁵⁹ God heard this and was filled with fury;
   God utterly rejected Israel,
⁶⁰ forsaking the dwelling place at Shiloh,
   the tent where God dwelt with human beings.
⁶¹ God gave the ark into captivity,
   divine splendor to the hands of the foe.

⁶² God gave up these people to the sword,
   showing anger against these chosen ones.
⁶³ So fire devoured their young men,
   their maidens had no wedding songs;
⁶⁴ their priests were cut down by the sword,
   and their widows made no lament.

⁶⁵ Then the Lord awoke as if from sleep,
   like a warrior maddened by wine,
⁶⁶ striking the foes from behind,
   and putting them to shame forever.

⁶⁷ The Lord rejected the tent of Joseph,
  and did not choose the tribe of Ephraim,
⁶⁸ but chose the tribe of Judah,
  the beloved mountain of Zion,
⁶⁹ building its shrine like the heavens,
  or like the earth which is founded forever.

⁷⁰ And God chose David as a servant,
  and took him away from the sheepfolds.
⁷¹ From the care of the ewes God brought him
  to be shepherd for the people of Jacob,
  over Israel, God's own possession.
⁷² He tended them with blameless heart;
  with his skillful hands he led them.

Psalm 79 *(78)*

¹ *A Psalm of Asaph.*

O God, the nations have invaded your heritage;
they have profaned your holy temple.
They have made Jerusalem a heap of ruins.
² They have handed over the bodies of your
servants
as food to feed the birds of heaven,
and the flesh of your faithful to the beasts of the
earth.

³ They have poured out their blood like water
round Jerusalem;
no one is left to bury the dead.
⁴ We have become the taunt of our neighbors,
the mockery and scorn of those around us.
⁵ How long, O Lord? Will you be angry forever?
Will your jealous anger burn like fire?

⁶ Pour out your rage on the nations,
those who do not know you,
peoples that do not call upon your name.
⁷ For they devoured the family of Jacob
and laid waste the place where they dwell.

8 Do not remember against us
    the guilt of former times.
    Let your compassion hasten to meet us;
    for we have been brought very low.

9 Help us, O God our savior,
    for the sake of the glory of your name.
    Free us and forgive us our sins,
    because of your name.

10 Why should the nations say, "Where is their
        God?"
    Before our eyes make it known among the
        nations
    that you avenge the blood of your servants that
        was shed.
11 Let the groans of the prisoners come before you,
    your strong arm reprieve those condemned to
        die.

12 Pay back to our neighbors seven times over
    the taunts with which they taunted you, O Lord.
13 Then we, your people, the flock of your pasture,
    will give you thanks forever and ever.
    From age to age we will recount your praise.

Psalm 80 *(79)*

¹ *For the Choirmaster. Intoned like "Lilies of*
   Testimony." Of Asaph. A Psalm.

² O shepherd of Israel, hear us,
   you who lead Joseph like a flock:
   enthroned on the cherubim, shine forth
³ upon Ephraim, Benjamin, Manasseh.
   Rouse up your might and come to save us.

⁴ Bring us back, O God;
   let your face shine forth, that we might be saved.

⁵ How long, O LORD, God of hosts,
   will you be angry at the prayer of your people?
⁶ You have fed them with tears for their bread,
   an abundance of tears for their drink.
⁷ You have made us the taunt of our neighbors;
   our foes mock us among themselves.

⁸ Bring us back, O God;
   let your face shine forth, that we might be saved.

⁹ You brought a vine out of Egypt;
   you drove out the nations and planted it.
¹⁰ Before it you cleared the ground;
   it took root and filled the land.

¹¹ The mountains were covered with its shadow,
the cedars of God with its boughs.
¹² It stretched out its branches to the sea;
to the River it stretched out its shoots.

¹³ Then why have you broken down its walls?
It is plucked by all who pass by the way.
¹⁴ It is ravaged by the boar of the forest,
devoured by the beasts of the field.

¹⁵ God of hosts, turn again, we implore;
look down from heaven and see.

Visit this vine and protect it,
¹⁶ the stock your right hand has planted,
the one you have claimed for yourself.
¹⁷ They have burnt it with fire and cut it down.
May they perish at the frown of your face.

¹⁸ May your hand be on the one at your right hand,
the one you have confirmed as your own.
¹⁹ And we shall never forsake you again;
give us life that we may call upon your name.

²⁰ Bring us back, O Lᴏʀᴅ God of hosts;
let your face shine forth, that we might be saved.

Psalm 81 (80)

¹ *For the Choirmaster. Upon the gittith. Of Asaph.*

² Sing joyfully to God our strength,
  shout in triumph to the God of Jacob.
³ Raise a song and sound the timbrel,
  the sweet-sounding lyre with the harp;
⁴ blow the trumpet at the new moon,
  when the moon is full, on our feast.

⁵ For this is a statute in Israel,
  a command of the God of Jacob,
⁶ who made it a decree for Joseph,
  when they went out from the land of Egypt.

A voice I did not know said to me:
⁷ "I freed your shoulder from the burden;
  your hands were freed from the builder's basket.
⁸ You called in distress and I delivered you.

"I answered, concealed in the thunder;
  at the waters of Meribah I tested you.
⁹ Listen, my people, as I warn you.
  O Israel, if only you would heed!

¹⁰ "Let there be no strange god among you,
   nor shall you worship a foreign god.
¹¹ I am the LORD your God,
   who brought you up from the land of Egypt.
   Open wide your mouth, and I will fill it.

¹² "But my people did not heed my voice,
   and Israel would not obey me.
¹³ So I left them in their stubbornness of heart,
   to follow their own designs.

¹⁴ "O that my people would heed me,
   that Israel would walk in my ways!
¹⁵ At once I would subdue their foes,
   turn my hand against their enemies.

¹⁶ "Those who hate the LORD would cringe,
   and their fate would last forever.
¹⁷ But Israel I would feed with finest wheat,
   and satisfy with honey from the rock."

Psalm 82 *(81)*

¹ *A Psalm of Asaph.*

God stands in the divine assembly,
in the midst of the gods gives judgment.

² "How long will you judge unjustly,
and favor the cause of the wicked?
³ Do justice for the weak and the orphan;
give justice to the poor and afflicted.
⁴ Rescue the weak and the needy;
set them free from the hand of the wicked."

⁵ They neither know nor understand;
they walk about in darkness,
and all the earth's foundations are shaken.

⁶ I have said to you, "You are gods,
and all of you, children of the Most High.
⁷ And yet, like human beings you shall die;
you shall fall, like any earthly ruler."

⁸ Arise, O God; judge the earth!
For all the nations are yours.

Psalm 83 *(82)*

¹ *A Song. A Psalm of Asaph.*

² O God, do not be silent;
  do not be still and unmoved, O God.
³ For your enemies raise a tumult;
  those who hate you lift up their heads.

⁴ They plot against your people,
  conspire against those you cherish.
⁵ They say, "Come, let us destroy them as a nation;
  let not the name of Israel be remembered."

⁶ They conspire with a single mind;
  against you they make a covenant:
⁷ the camps of Edom and of Ishmael,
  of Moab and Hagar,

⁸ Gebal and Ammon and Amalek,
  Philistia, with the people of Tyre.
⁹ Assyria, too, is their ally,
  and joins hands with the children of Lot.

¹⁰ Treat them like Midian, like Sisera,
  like Jabin at the River Kishon,
¹¹ those who were destroyed at Endor,
  whose bodies rotted on the ground.

¹² Make their captains like Oreb and Zeeb,
   all their princes like Zebah and Zalmunna,
¹³ who said, "Let us take the fields of God
   and make them our own possession."

¹⁴ My God, scatter them like the whirlwind,
   drive them like chaff in the wind!
¹⁵ As fire that burns away the forest,
   as the flame that sets the mountains ablaze,
¹⁶ drive them away with your tempest,
   and fill them with terror at your storm.

¹⁷ Cover their faces with shame,
   so that they seek your name, O LORD.
¹⁸ Shame and terror be theirs forever.
   Let them be disgraced; let them perish!

¹⁹ Let them know that you alone,
   you whose name is the LORD,
   are the Most High over all the earth.

Psalm 84 *(83)*

¹ *For the Choirmaster. Upon the gittith. Of the sons*
   of Korah. A Psalm.

² How lovely is your dwelling place,
   O LORD of hosts.
³ My soul is longing and yearning
   for the courts of the LORD.
   My heart and my flesh cry out
   to the living God.

⁴ Even the sparrow finds a home,
   and the swallow a nest for herself
   in which she sets her young, at your altars,
   O LORD of hosts, my king and my God.

⁵ Blessed are they who dwell in your house,
   forever singing your praise.
⁶ Blessed the people whose strength is in you,
   whose hearts are set on the pilgrimage.

⁷ As they go through the Baca Valley,
   they make it a place of springs;
   the autumn rain covers it with pools.
⁸ They walk with ever-growing strength;
   the God of gods will appear in Zion.

⁹ O LORD, God of hosts, hear my prayer;
   give ear, O God of Jacob.
¹⁰ Behold our shield, O God;
   look on the face of your anointed.

¹¹ One day within your courts
   is better than a thousand elsewhere.
   The threshold of the house of my God
   I prefer to the tents of the wicked.

¹² For the LORD God is a sun, a shield;
   the LORD will give us favor and glory,
   And will not withhold any good
   from those who walk without blame.
¹³ O LORD of hosts, how blessed
   is the one who trusts in you!

Psalm 85 (84)

¹ *For the Choirmaster. Of the sons of Korah. A Psalm.*

² O LORD, you have favored your land,
and brought back the captives of Jacob.
³ You forgave the guilt of your people,
and covered all their sins.
⁴ You averted all your rage;
you turned back the heat of your anger.

⁵ Bring us back, O God, our savior!
Put an end to your grievance against us.
⁶ Will you be angry with us forever?
Will your anger last from age to age?

⁷ Will you not restore again our life,
that your people may rejoice in you?
⁸ Show us, O LORD, your mercy,
and grant us your salvation.

⁹ I will hear what the LORD God speaks,
who speaks of peace to his faithful people,
and those who turn to God in their hearts.
¹⁰ For those who fear God, salvation is near,
and the Lord's glory will dwell in our land.

[11] Merciful love and faithfulness have met;
righteousness and peace have kissed.
[12] Faithfulness shall spring from the earth,
and righteousness look down from heaven.

[13] Also the LORD will bestow a great bounty,
and our earth shall yield its increase.
[14] Righteousness will march as a vanguard,
and guide God's steps on the way.

Psalm 86 *(85)*

¹ *A Prayer of David.*

Turn your ear, O LORD, and answer me,
  for I am poor and needy.
² Preserve my soul, for I am faithful;
  save the servant who trusts in you, my God.

³ Have mercy on me, O Lord,
  for I cry to you all the day long.
⁴ Gladden the soul of your servant,
  for I lift up my soul to you, O Lord.

⁵ O Lord, you are good and forgiving,
  full of mercy to all who call to you.
⁶ Give ear, O LORD, to my prayer,
  and attend to my voice in supplication.

⁷ In the day of distress, I will call to you,
  and surely you will answer me.
⁸ Among the gods there is none like you, O Lord,
  nor works to compare with yours.

⁹ All the nations you have made shall come;
  they will bow down before you, O Lord,
  and glorify your name,
¹⁰ for you are great and do marvelous deeds,
  you who alone are God.

¹¹ Teach me, O Lord, your way,
   so that I may walk in your truth,
   single-heartedly revering your name.

¹² I will praise you, Lord my God, with all my
       heart,
   and glorify your name forever.
¹³ Your faithful love to me has been great;
   you have saved me from the depths of Sheol.

¹⁴ The proud have risen against me, O God;
   a band of the ruthless seeks my life.
   To you they pay no heed.

¹⁵ But you, O God, are compassionate and
       gracious,
   slow to anger, O Lord,
   abundant in love and fidelity;
¹⁶ turn and take pity on me.

   O give your strength to your servant,
   and save the child of your handmaid.
¹⁷ Show me the sign of your favor,
   that my foes may see to their shame
   that you, O Lord, give me comfort and help.

Psalm 87 (86)

¹ *Of the sons of Korah. A Psalm. A Song.*

Founded by God on the holy mountain,
² the LORD loves the gates of Zion,
 more than all the dwellings of Jacob.
³ Of you are told glorious things,
 you, O city of God!

⁴ "Rahab and Babylon I will count
 among those who know me;
 Of Tyre, Philistia, Ethiopia, it is told,
 'There was this one born.'
⁵ But of Zion it shall be said,
 'Each one was born in her.'"

God, the Most High, will establish her.
⁶ In the register of peoples the LORD writes,
 "Here was this one born."
⁷ The singers cry out in chorus,
 "All my wellsprings are in you."

Psalm 88 (87)

¹ *A Song. A Psalm. Of the sons of Korah. For the*
Choirmaster. Intoned like Mahalat Leannoth.
A Maskil. *For Heman the Ezrahite.*

² O LORD and God of my salvation,
I cry before you day and night.
³ Let my prayer come forth to your presence.
Incline your ear to my cry.
⁴ For my soul is filled with evils;
my life is on the brink of Sheol.

⁵ I am reckoned as one who goes down to the pit;
I am like a warrior without strength,
⁶ like one roaming among the dead,
like the slain who lie in the grave,
like those you remember no more,
cut off, as they are, from your hand.

⁷ You have laid me in the depths of the pit,
in regions that are dark and deep.
⁸ Your anger weighs down upon me;
I am drowned beneath your waves.
⁹ You have taken away my friends;
to them you have made me hateful.

Imprisoned, I cannot escape;
¹⁰ my eyes are sunken with grief.
I call to you, LORD, all day long;
to you I stretch out my hands.

¹¹ Will you work your wonders for the dead?
Will the shades rise up to praise you?
¹² From the grave, who can tell of your love?
From the place of perdition your faithfulness?
¹³ Will your wonders be known in the dark,
in the land of oblivion your righteousness?

¹⁴ But I, O LORD, cry out to you;
in the morning my prayer comes before you.
¹⁵ Why do you reject me, O LORD?
Why do you hide your face from me?

¹⁶ I am wretched, close to death from my youth.
I have borne your trials; I am numb.
¹⁷ Your fury has swept down upon me;
your terrors have utterly destroyed me.

¹⁸ They surround me all the day like a flood;
together they close in against me.
¹⁹ Friend and neighbor you have taken away:
my one companion is darkness.

Psalm 89 *(88)*

¹ *A* Maskil. *For Ethan the Ezrahite.*

² I will sing of your faithful love, O Lᴏʀᴅ, forever;
  through all ages my mouth will proclaim your
     fidelity.
³ I have declared your faithful love is established
     forever;
  your fidelity stands firm as the heavens.

⁴ "With my chosen one I have made a covenant;
  I have sworn to David my servant:
⁵ I will establish your descendants forever,
  and set up your throne through all ages."

⁶ The heavens praise your wonders, O Lᴏʀᴅ,
  your fidelity, too, in the assembly of your holy
     ones.
⁷ For who in the skies can compare with the Lᴏʀᴅ,
  or who is like the Lᴏʀᴅ among the heavenly
     powers?
⁸ A God to be feared in the council of the holy
     ones,
  great and awesome above all around him.

⁹ O Lᴏʀᴅ God of hosts, who is your equal?
  You are mighty, O Lᴏʀᴅ, and fidelity surrounds
      you.
¹⁰ It is you who rule the raging of the sea;
  it is you who still the surging of its waves.
¹¹ It is you who crush Rahab underfoot like a
      corpse;
  you scatter your foes with your mighty arm.

¹² The heavens are yours, the earth is yours;
  you have founded the world and its fullness;
¹³ it is you who created the North and the South.
  Tabor and Hermon shout for joy at your name.

¹⁴ Yours is a mighty arm.
  Your hand is strong; your right hand is exalted.
¹⁵ Righteousness and justice are the pillars of your
      throne;
  loving kindness and fidelity walk in your presence.

¹⁶ How blessed the people who know your praise,
  who walk, O Lᴏʀᴅ, in the light of your face,
¹⁷ who find their joy every day in your name,
  who make your righteousness their joyful
      acclaim.

¹⁸ For you are the glory of their strength;
  by your favor it is that our might is exalted;
¹⁹ Behold, the Lᴏʀᴅ is our shield,
  the Holy One of Israel, our king.

20 Then you spoke in a vision.
   To your faithful ones you said,
   "I have bestowed my help on a warrior,
   I have exalted one chosen from the people.

21 "I have found my servant David,
   and with my holy oil anointed him.
22 My hand shall always be with him,
   and my arm shall make him strong.

23 "The enemy shall never outwit him,
   nor shall the son of iniquity humble him.
24 I will beat down his foes before him,
   and those who hate him I will strike.

25 "My love and my faithfulness shall be with him;
   by my name his might shall be exalted.
26 I will stretch out his hand to the Sea,
   and his right hand upon the Rivers.

27 "He will call out to me, 'You are my father,
   my God, the rock of my salvation.'
28 I for my part will make him my firstborn,
   the highest of the kings of the earth.

29 "I will keep my faithful love for him always;
   with him my covenant shall last.
30 I will establish his descendants forever,
   and his throne as lasting as the days of heaven.

³¹ "If his descendants forsake my law
  and refuse to walk as I decree,
³² and if ever they violate my statutes,
  failing to keep my commands:

³³ "Then I will punish their offenses with the rod;
  then I will scourge them on account of their
      guilt.
³⁴ But I will never take back my love;
  my fidelity will never fail.
³⁵ I will never violate my covenant,
  nor go back on the promise of my lips.

³⁶ "Once for all, I have sworn by my holiness.
  'I will never lie to David.
³⁷ His descendants shall continue forever.
  In my sight his throne is like the sun;
³⁸ like the moon, it shall endure forever,
  a faithful witness in the heavens.'"

³⁹ But yet you have spurned and rejected,
  you are angry with the one you have anointed.
⁴⁰ You have renounced your covenant with your
      servant,
  and dishonored his crown in the dust.

⁴¹ You have broken down all his walls,
  and reduced his fortresses to ruins.
⁴² All who pass by despoil him;
  he has become the taunt of his neighbors.

⁴³ You have exalted the right hand of his foes;
   you have made all his enemies rejoice.
⁴⁴ You have turned back the edge of his sword;
   you have not upheld him in battle.

⁴⁵ You have brought his glory to an end;
   you have hurled his throne to the ground.
⁴⁶ You have cut short the days of his youth;
   you have heaped disgrace upon him.

⁴⁷ How long, O Lᴏʀᴅ? Will you hide yourself
      forever?
   How long will your anger burn like a fire?
⁴⁸ Remember the shortness of my life,
   and how frail you have made the human race.
⁴⁹ Who can live and never see death?
   Who can save themselves from the grasp of Sheol?

⁵⁰ Where are your mercies of the past, O Lord,
   which you swore in your faithfulness to David?
⁵¹ Remember, O Lord, the taunts to your servant,
   how I bear in my breast the scorn of many
      peoples.
⁵² Thus your enemies lift up a taunt, O Lᴏʀᴅ,
   taunting your anointed at every step.

*   *   *

[53] Blest be the Lᴏʀᴅ forever.
   Amen and amen!

BOOK FOUR
OF THE PSALTER

Psalm 90 (89)

¹ *Prayer of Moses, the man of God.*

O Lord, you have been our refuge,
  from generation to generation.
² Before the mountains were born,
  or the earth or the world were brought forth,
  you are God, from age to age.

³ You turn human beings back to dust,
  and say, "Return, O children of Adam."
⁴ To your eyes a thousand years
  are like yesterday, come and gone,
  or like a watch in the night.

⁵ You sweep them away like a dream,
  like grass which is fresh in the morning.
⁶ In the morning it sprouts and is fresh;
  by evening it withers and fades.

⁷ Indeed, we are consumed by your anger;
  we are struck with terror at your fury.
⁸ You have set our guilt before you,
  our secret sins in the light of your face.

⁹ All our days pass away in your anger.
  Our years are consumed like a sigh.
¹⁰ Seventy years is the span of our days,
  or eighty if we are strong.
  And most of these are toil and pain.
  They pass swiftly and we are gone.

¹¹ Who understands the power of your anger?
  Your fury matches the fear of you.
¹² Then teach us to number our days,
  that we may gain wisdom of heart.

¹³ Turn back, O LORD! How long?
  Show pity to your servants.
¹⁴ At dawn, fill us with your faithful love;
  we shall exult and rejoice all our days.
¹⁵ Give us joy for the days of our affliction,
  for the years when we looked upon evil.

¹⁶ Let your deed be seen by your servants,
  and your glorious power by their children.
¹⁷ Let the favor of the LORD our God be upon us;
  give success to the work of our hands.
  O give success to the work of our hands.

Psalm 91 (90)

1 You who dwell in the Most High's hidden place,
  and abide in the shade of the Almighty,
2 say to the LORD, "My refuge,
  my stronghold, my God in whom I trust!"

3 The Lord will free you from the snare of the
    fowler,
  from the destructive plague.
4 The pinions of God will conceal you,
  under wings of the Lord you will find refuge.
  God's faithfulness is buckler and shield.

5 You will not fear the terror of the night,
  nor the arrow that flies by day,
6 nor the plague that prowls in the darkness,
  nor the scourge that lays waste at noon.

7 A thousand may fall at your side,
  ten thousand fall at your right:
  you it will never approach.

8 Your eyes have only to look
  to see how the wicked are repaid.
9 For you, O LORD, are my refuge.
  You have made the Most High your dwelling.

¹⁰ Upon you no evil shall fall,
   no plague approach your tent.
¹¹ For you has God commanded the angels
   to keep you in all your ways.

¹² They shall bear you upon their hands,
   lest you strike your foot against a stone.
¹³ On the lion and the viper you will tread,
   and trample the young lion and the serpent.

¹⁴ Since you cling to me in love, I will free you,
   protect you, for you know my name.
¹⁵ When you call on me, I will answer you;
   I will be with you in distress;
   I will deliver you, and give you glory.

¹⁶ With length of days I will content you;
   I will show you my saving power.

Psalm 92 (91)

¹ *A Psalm. A Song for the Sabbath.*

² It is good to give thanks to the Lord,
   to make music to your name, O Most High,
³ to proclaim your faithful love in the morning,
   and your truth in the watches of the night,
⁴ on the ten-stringed lute and the harp,
   with the sound of song on the lyre.

⁵ You have gladdened me, O Lord, by your deeds;
   for the work of your hands I shout with joy.
⁶ O Lord, how great are your works!
   How deep are your designs!
⁷ The senseless cannot know this,
   and the fool cannot understand.

⁸ Though the wicked spring up like grass,
   and all who do evil thrive,
      they are doomed to be eternally destroyed.
⁹ But you, O Lord, are eternally on high.

¹⁰ See, your enemies, O Lord,
    see, your enemies will perish;
    all who do evil will be scattered.

¹¹ You give me the strength of a wild ox;
    you have poured out on me purest oil.
¹² My eyes looked in triumph on my foes;
    my ears have heard of their fall.

¹³ The righteous will flourish like the palm tree,
   and grow like a Lebanon cedar.

¹⁴ Planted in the house of the LORD,
   they will flourish in the courts of our God,
¹⁵ still bearing fruit when they are old,
   still full of sap, still green,
¹⁶ to proclaim that the LORD is upright.
   In God, my rock, there is no wrong.

Psalm 93 (92)

¹ The LORD is king, with majesty enrobed.
   The LORD is robed with might,
   and girded round about with power.

   The world you made firm, not to be moved;
² your throne has stood firm from of old.
   From all eternity, O LORD, you are.

³ The floods have lifted up, O LORD,
   the floods have lifted up their voice;
   the floods have lifted up their thunder.

⁴ Greater than the roar of mighty waters,
   mightier than the surgings of the sea,
   the LORD is mighty on high.

⁵ Truly your decrees are to be trusted.
   Holiness is fitting to your house,
   O LORD, until the end of time.

Psalm 94 (93)

1 O Lᴏʀᴅ, avenging God,
   avenging God, shine forth!
2 Judge of the earth, arise;
   give the proud what they deserve!

3 How long, O Lᴏʀᴅ, shall the wicked,
   how long shall the wicked triumph?
4 They bluster with arrogant speech;
   those who do evil boast to each other.

5 They crush your people, Lᴏʀᴅ;
   and they humble your inheritance.
6 They kill the widow and the stranger,
   and murder the orphaned child.

7 And they say, "The Lᴏʀᴅ does not see;
   the God of Jacob pays no heed."
8 Mark this, you senseless people;
   fools, when will you understand?

9 Can the One who planted the ear not hear?
   Can the One who formed the eye not see?
10 Will the One who trains the nations not punish?
    Will the One who teaches us not have knowledge?
11 The Lᴏʀᴅ knows the plans of human beings,
    knows they are no more than a breath.

¹² Blessed are they whom you discipline, O Lord,
    whom you train by means of your law;
¹³ to whom you give peace in evil days,
    while the pit is being dug for the wicked.

¹⁴ The Lord will not forsake the chosen people,
    nor abandon those who are God's inheritance;
¹⁵ for judgment shall again be righteous,
    and all upright hearts shall uphold it.

¹⁶ Who will stand up for me against the wicked?
    Who will defend me from those who do evil?
¹⁷ If the Lord were not to help me,
    my soul would soon go down to the silence.

¹⁸ When I think, "I have lost my foothold,"
    your faithful love, O Lord, upholds me.
¹⁹ When cares increase in my heart,
    your consolation calms my soul.

²⁰ Can judges who do evil be your friends?
    They do injustice under cover of law;
²¹ they attack the life of the righteous,
    and condemn the innocent to death.

²² As for me, the Lord will be a stronghold;
    my God will be the rock where I take refuge.
²³ God will repay them for their wickedness,
    destroy them for their evil deeds.
    The Lord, our God, will destroy them.

Psalm 95 (94)

¹ Come, let us ring out our joy to the LORD;
  hail the rock who saves us.
² Let us come before God giving thanks;
  with songs of praise, let us hail the Lord.

³ A mighty God is the LORD,
  a great king above all gods,
⁴ in whose hand are the depths of the earth,
  and the heights of the mountains as well.
⁵ The sea belongs to God, who made it,
  whose hand shaped the dry land as well.

⁶ O come; let us bow and bend low.
  Let us kneel before the LORD who made us,
⁷ for the Lord is our God, and we
  the people of the heavenly pasture,
  the flock led by the almighty hand.

O that today you would heed God's voice!
8 "Harden not your hearts as at Meribah,
   as on that day at Massah in the desert
9 when your ancestors put me to the test;
   when they tried me, though they saw my work.

10 "For forty years I abhorred that generation,
   and I said, 'Their heart goes astray;
   this people does not know my ways.'
11 Then I took an oath in my anger,
   'Never shall they enter my rest.'"

Psalm 96 *(95)*

¹ O sing a new song to the Lord;
  sing to the Lord, all the earth.
² O sing to the Lord; bless God's name.
  Proclaim divine salvation day by day.
³ Tell among the nations God's glory,
  divine wonders among all the peoples.

⁴ For the Lord is great and highly to be praised,
  to be feared above all gods.
⁵ For the idols of the nations are naught.
  It was the Lord who made the heavens.
⁶ Greatness and splendor abound in God's presence,
  strength and honor in the holy place.

⁷ Ascribe to the Lord, you families of peoples,
  Ascribe to the Lord glory and power;
⁸ Ascribe to the Lord the glory of God's name.

  Bring an offering and enter God's courts;
⁹ worship the Lord in holy splendor.
  O tremble before God, all the earth.

¹⁰ Say to the nations, "The LORD is king,"
   who made firm the world in its place,
   and who will judge the peoples in fairness.

¹¹ Let the heavens rejoice and earth be glad;
   let the sea and all within it thunder praise.
¹² Let the field and all it bears rejoice.

   Then all the trees of the wood will shout for joy
¹³ at the presence of the LORD who comes;
   God comes to judge the earth.
   The Lord will judge the world with righteousness,
   and the peoples with faithfulness.

Psalm 97 (96)

¹ The LORD reigns, let earth rejoice;
 let the many islands be glad.
² Cloud and darkness surround the Lord,
 whose throne is founded on justice and right.

³ A fire prepares the pathway of God;
 it burns up the Lord's foes on every side.
⁴ God's lightnings light up the world;
 while the earth looks on and trembles.

⁵ The mountains melt like wax
 before the face of the LORD,
 before the face of the Lord of all the earth.
⁶ The skies proclaim divine righteousness;
 all peoples see the glory of God.

⁷ Let those who serve idols be ashamed,
 those who boast of their worthless gods.
 All you angels, worship the Lord.

⁸ Zion hears and is glad;
 the cities of Judah rejoice
 because of your judgments, O LORD.

⁹ For you indeed are the LORD
 most high above all the earth,
 exalted far above all gods.

¹⁰ The LORD loves those who hate evil,
  guards the souls of the faithful,
  and sets them free from the wicked.

¹¹ Light shines forth for the righteous,
  and joy for the upright of heart.
¹² Rejoice in the LORD, you righteous;
  in memory of God's holiness give thanks.

Psalm 98 (97)

¹ *A Psalm.*

O sing a new song to the LORD,
  who has worked such wonders,
  whose right hand and holy arm
  have brought salvation.

² The LORD has made known salvation,
  has shown deliverance to the nations.
³ God has remembered faithful love
  and truth for the house of Israel.

All the ends of the earth have seen
  the salvation of our God.
⁴ Shout to the LORD, all the earth;
  break forth into joyous song,
  and sing out your praise.

⁵ Sing psalms to the LORD with the harp,
  with the harp and the sound of song.
⁶ With trumpets and the sound of the horn,
  raise a shout before the King, the LORD.

⁷ Let the sea and all within it thunder;
  the world, and those who dwell in it.
⁸ Let the rivers clap their hands,
  and the hills ring out their joy
⁹ at the presence of the LORD who comes,
  who comes to judge the earth.
  The Lord will judge the world with righteousness,
  and the peoples with fairness.

Psalm 99 (98)

1 The LORD is king; the peoples tremble.
   God is enthroned on the cherubim; earth quakes.
2 The LORD is great in Zion,
   exalted over all the peoples.

3 Let them praise your great and awesome name,
   for the Lord our God is holy!
4 O mighty Ruler, lover of justice,
   you have established what is upright;
   you have made justice and right in Jacob.

5 Exalt the LORD our God;
   bow down before God's footstool,
   for the Lord our God is holy!

6 Among God's priests were Aaron and Moses;
   among those who invoked God's name was Samuel.
   They cried out to the LORD, who answered.

7 To them the Lord spoke in the pillar of cloud.
   They obeyed the decrees and the statutes
   which the Lord had given them.

8 O LORD our God, you answered them.
   For them you were a God who forgives,
   and yet you punished their offenses.

9 Exalt the LORD our God;
   bow down before the holy mountain,
   for the LORD our God is holy.

Psalm 100 (99)

¹ *A Psalm of Thanksgiving.*

Cry out with joy to the Lord, all the earth.
² Serve the Lord with gladness.
Come before God, singing for joy.

³ Know that the Lord is God,
who made us, to whom we belong.
We are God's people, the sheep of God's flock.

⁴ Enter the temple gates with thanksgiving
and its courts with songs of praise.
Give thanks and bless God's name.

⁵ Indeed, how good is the Lord,
eternal God's merciful love.
God is faithful from age to age.

Psalm 101 (100)

¹ *Of David. A Psalm.*

I sing of faithful love and justice;
I raise a psalm to you, O Lord.
² I will ponder the way of the blameless.
O when will you come to me?

I will walk with blameless heart
within my house;
³ I will not set before my eyes
whatever is base.

I hate the deeds of the crooked;
such I will not endure.
⁴ The false-hearted must keep far away;
I will know no evil.

⁵ The one who slanders a neighbor in secret
I will bring to silence.
Proud eyes and haughty heart
I will never endure.

⁶ My eyes are on the faithful of the land,
that they may dwell with me.
The one who walks in the way of the blameless
shall be my servant.

⁷ No one who practices deceit
shall live within my house.
No one who utters lies
shall stand before my eyes.

⁸ Morning by morning I will subdue
all the wicked in the land,
uprooting from the city of the LORD
all who do evil.

Psalm 102 (101)

¹ *Prayer of someone afflicted who is weary and pours out his trouble to the* LORD.

² Hear my prayer, O LORD,
  and let my cry come to you.
³ Do not hide your face from me
  in the day of my distress.
  Turn your ear towards me;
  on the day when I call,
  speedily answer me.

⁴ For my days are vanishing like smoke;
  my bones burn away like a furnace.
⁵ My heart is withered and dried up like the grass.
  I forget to eat my bread.
⁶ Because of the sound of my groaning,
  my bones hold fast to my flesh.

⁷ I have become like a vulture in the desert,
  like an owl among the ruins.
⁸ I lie awake and I moan,
  like a bird alone on a roof.
⁹ All day long my foes revile me;
  those who deride me use my name as a curse.

¹⁰ I have eaten ashes like bread,
and mingled tears with my drink.
¹¹ Because of your anger and fury,
you have lifted me up and thrown me down.
¹² My days are like a fading shadow,
and I wither away like the grass.

¹³ But you, O LORD, are enthroned forever,
and your renown is from age to age.

¹⁴ You will arise and take pity on Zion,
for this is the time to have mercy;
yes, the time appointed has come.
¹⁵ Behold, your servants love her very stones,
are moved to pity for her dust.

¹⁶ The nations shall fear the name of the LORD,
and all the earth's kings your glory,
¹⁷ when the LORD shall build up Zion,
and appear in all divine glory.
¹⁸ God will turn to the prayers of the helpless;
and will not despise their prayers.

¹⁹ Let this be written for ages to come,
that a people yet unborn may praise the LORD;
²⁰ The LORD looked down from the holy place on
high,
looked down from heaven to the earth,
²¹ to hear the groans of the prisoners,
and free those condemned to die.

²² May the name of the LORD be proclaimed in
        Zion,
    and praised in Jerusalem,
²³ when peoples and kingdoms are gathered as one
    to offer their worship to the LORD.

²⁴ The Lord has broken my strength in midcourse,
    and has shortened my days.
²⁵ I say: "My God, do not take me away
    before half of my days are complete,
    you, whose days last from age to age.

²⁶ Long ago you founded the earth,
    and the heavens are the work of your hands.
²⁷ They will perish but you will remain.
    They will all wear out like a garment.
    You will change them like clothes, and they
        change.
²⁸ But you are the same, and your years do not
        end."

²⁹ The children of your servants shall dwell
        untroubled,
    and their descendants established before you.

Psalm 103 (102)

¹ *Of David.*

Bless the LORD, O my soul,
and all within me, the holy name of God.
² Bless the LORD, O my soul,
and never forget all God's benefits.

³ It is the Lord who forgives all your sins,
who heals every one of your ills,
⁴ who redeems your life from the grave,
who crowns you with love and compassion,
⁵ who fills your life with good things,
renewing your youth like an eagle's.

⁶ The LORD does righteous deeds,
gives full justice to all who are oppressed.
⁷ The Lord made known divine ways to Moses,
and wondrous deeds to the children of Israel.

⁸ The LORD is compassionate and gracious,
slow to anger and abounding in love,
⁹ not always finding fault,
nor persisting in anger forever.
¹⁰ God does not treat us according to our sins,
nor repay us according to our faults.

¹¹ For as the heavens are high above the earth,
　　so strong the mercy for those who fear God.
¹² As far as the east is from the west,
　　so far from us does God remove our
　　　transgressions.

¹³ As a father has compassion on his children,
　　divine compassion is on those who fear the LORD,
¹⁴ who knows of what we are made,
　　who remembers that we are dust.

¹⁵ Human beings, their days are like grass;
　　they flower like the flower of the field.
¹⁶ The wind blows, and it is no more,
　　and its place never sees it again.

¹⁷ But the love of the LORD is everlasting
　　upon those who revere godly ways,
　　upon children's children divine righteousness
¹⁸ for those who keep the covenant,
　　and remember to fulfill its commands.

¹⁹ The LORD has fixed a throne in heaven,
   and God's kingdom is ruling over all.
²⁰ Bless the LORD, all you angels of heaven,
   mighty in power, fulfilling God's word,
   who heed the voice of God's word.

²¹ Bless the LORD, all you hosts,
   you servants, who do God's will.
²² Bless the LORD, all you creatures,
   in every place of God's domain.
   Bless the LORD, O my soul!

Psalm 104 (103)

¹ Bless the LORD, O my soul!
  O LORD my God, how great you are,
  clothed in majesty and honor,
² wrapped in light as with a robe!

  You stretch out the heavens like a tent;
³ you lay beams on the waters for your dwelling.
  You make the clouds your chariot;
  you ride on the wings of the wind.
⁴ You make the winds your messengers,
  flame and fire your servants.

⁵ You set the earth on its foundation,
  immovable from age to age.
⁶ You wrapped it with the depths like a cloak;
  the waters stood higher than the mountains.
⁷ At your threat they took to flight;
  at the voice of your thunder they fled.

⁸ The mountains rose, the valleys descended
  to the place which you had appointed them.
⁹ You set limits they might not pass,
  lest the depths return to cover the earth.

¹⁰ You make springs gush forth in the valleys;
   they flow in between the hills.
¹¹ They give drink to all the beasts of the field;
   the wild asses quench their thirst.
¹² There the birds of heaven build their nests;
   from the branches they sing their song.

¹³ From your dwelling you water the mountains;
   by your works the earth has its fill.

¹⁴ You make the grass grow for the cattle
   and plants to serve human needs,
   to bring forth bread from the earth,
¹⁵ and wine to cheer people's hearts;
   oil, to make faces shine,
   and bread to strengthen the human heart.

¹⁶ The trees of the LORD drink their fill,
   and the cedars planted on Lebanon;
¹⁷ there the birds build their nests;
   on the treetop the stork has a home.
¹⁸ For the goats the lofty mountains,
   for the rabbits the rocks are a refuge.

¹⁹ You made the moon to mark the months;
   the sun knows the time for its setting.
²⁰ You spread the darkness, it is night,
   and all the beasts of the forest creep forth.
²¹ The young lions roar for their prey,
   and seek their food from God.

²² At the rising of the sun they steal away;
   and they go to lie down in their dens.
²³ People go forth to their work,
   to labor till evening falls.

²⁴ How many are your works, O LORD!
   In wisdom you have made them all.
   The earth is full of your creatures.

²⁵ Vast and wide is the span of the sea,
   with its creeping things past counting,
   living things great and small.
²⁶ The ships are moving there,
   and Leviathan you made to play with.

²⁷ All of these look to you
   to give them their food in due season.
²⁸ You give it, they gather it up;
   you open wide your hand, they are well filled.

²⁹ You hide your face, they are dismayed;
   you take away their breath, they die,
   returning to the dust from which they came.
³⁰ When you send forth your breath, they are
      created,
   and you renew the face of the earth.

³¹ May the glory of the LORD last forever!
   May the LORD rejoice in these works!
³² God looks on the earth and it trembles;
   touches the mountains and they smoke.

³³ I will sing to the LORD all my life,
   sing psalms to my God while I live.
³⁴ May my thoughts be pleasing to God.
   I will rejoice in the LORD.

³⁵ Let sinners vanish from the earth,
   and the wicked exist no more.
   Bless the LORD, O my soul.

Alleluia!

Psalm 105 (104)

¹ Give thanks and proclaim the name of the LORD;
  make known God's deeds among the peoples.

² O sing to God, sing praise;
  tell all the wonderful works of the Lord!
³ Glory in the holy name of God;
  let hearts that seek the LORD rejoice.

⁴ Turn to the LORD who is strong;
  constantly seek God's face.
⁵ Remember the wonders the Lord has done,
  great marvels and words of judgment.

⁶ O children of Abraham, God's servant,
  O descendants of Jacob the chosen one,
⁷ it is the LORD who is our God,
  whose judgments are in all the earth.

⁸ The Lord remembers the covenant forever:
  the promise ordained for a thousand generations,
⁹ the covenant made with Abraham,
  the oath that was sworn to Isaac.

¹⁰ God confirmed it for Jacob as a law,
  for Israel as a covenant forever:
¹¹ "I will give you the land of Canaan
  to be your allotted inheritance."

¹² When they were few in number,
   a handful of strangers in the land,
¹³ when they wandered from nation to nation,
   from one kingdom and people to another,

¹⁴ God allowed no one to oppress them;
   and admonished kings on their account,
¹⁵ saying, "Those I have anointed, do not touch;
   do no harm to any of my prophets."

¹⁶ But a famine was called down on the land;
   their staff of bread was broken.
¹⁷ God had sent a man ahead of them,
   Joseph, sold as a slave.

¹⁸ His feet were weighed down in chains,
   his neck was bound with iron,
¹⁹ until what God said came to pass,
   and the word of the LORD proved him true.

²⁰ Then the king sent orders and released him;
   the ruler of the peoples set him free.
²¹ He made him master of his house
   and ruler of all his possessions,
²² to instruct his princes from his heart,
   and to teach his elders wisdom.

²³ So Israel came into Egypt;
  Jacob sojourned in the land of Ham.
²⁴ The Lord gave this people great increase,
  and made them stronger than their foes,
²⁵ whose hearts were turned to hate the Lord's
    people,
  and to deal with deceit toward God's servants.

²⁶ Then Moses, God's servant, was sent,
  and Aaron whom God had chosen.
²⁷ They performed great signs among them,
  and wonders in the land of Ham.

²⁸ God sent darkness, and darkness came,
  but they rebelled against the words of God;
²⁹ the Lord turned their waters into blood,
  and caused their fish to die.

³⁰ Their land was overrun by frogs,
  even to the halls of their kings.
³¹ God spoke; there came swarms of flies,
  and gnats covered all the country.

³² In place of the rain there came hailstones,
  and lightning flashing in their land;
³³ God struck their vines and fig trees,
  and shattered the trees through their country.

³⁴ God spoke; the locusts came forth,
   young locusts, too many to be counted.
³⁵ They ate up every plant in the land;
   they ate up all the fruit of their fields.

³⁶ All the firstborn in their land were struck,
   the first fruit of all their strength.
³⁷ God led out Israel with silver and gold.
   In the tribes were none who stumbled.

³⁸ Egypt rejoiced when they left,
   for dread had fallen upon them.
³⁹ God spread a cloud as a screen,
   and fire to illumine the night.

⁴⁰ When they asked, the Lord sent them quails,
   and filled them with bread from heaven.
⁴¹ The rock was pierced and water gushed forth;
   in the desert it flowed as a river.

⁴² For God remembered the holy word
   spoken to Abraham, servant of the Lord,
⁴³ God brought out the people with joy,
   the chosen ones with shouts of rejoicing.

⁴⁴ The Lord gave them the lands of the nations.
   They inherited the fruits of the peoples' toil,
⁴⁵ that thus they might keep divine precepts,
   that thus they might observe God's laws.

Alleluia!

Psalm 106 (105)

[1] Alleluia!

O give thanks to the LORD, who is good,
whose faithful love endures forever.
[2] Who can tell the LORD's mighty deeds,
or recount God's praise in full?

[3] Blessed are they who observe what is just,
who at all times do what is righteous.
[4] O LORD, remember me
with the favor you show to your people.

Visit me with your saving power,
[5] that I may see the riches of your chosen ones,
and may rejoice in the gladness of your nation,
boasting in the glory of your heritage.

[6] Like our forebears, we have sinned.
We have done wrong; our deeds have been evil.
[7] Our forebears, when they were in Egypt,
did not grasp the meaning of your wonders.

They forgot the great number of your mercies,
at the Red Sea they defied the Most High.
[8] Yet you saved them for the sake of your name,
in order to make known your power.

⁹ You rebuked the Red Sea; it dried up,
    and you led them through the deep as through
        the desert.
¹⁰ You saved them from the hand of the foe;
    and freed them from the grip of the enemy.

¹¹ The waters covered their oppressors;
    not one of them was left.
¹² Then they believed in your words;
    then they sang your praises.

¹³ But they soon forgot your deeds,
    and would not wait upon your counsel.
¹⁴ They yielded to their cravings in the desert,
    and put God to the test in the wilderness.

¹⁵ You granted them the favor they asked,
    but struck them with a wasting disease.
¹⁶ In the camp, they were jealous of Moses,
    and also Aaron, who was holy to the Lord.

¹⁷ The earth opened and swallowed up Dathan,
    and buried the clan of Abiram.
¹⁸ Fire blazed up against their clan,
    and flames devoured the wicked.

¹⁹ They fashioned a calf at Horeb,
    and worshiped an image of metal;
²⁰ they exchanged their glory
    for the image of a bull that eats grass.

²¹ They forgot the God who was their savior,
    who had done such great things in Egypt,
²² such wonders in the land of Ham,
    such awesome deeds at the Red Sea.

²³ For this God threatened to destroy them,
    but Moses, the man God had chosen,
    stood in the breach before them,
    to turn back God's anger from destruction.

²⁴ Then they scorned the desirable land;
    they had no faith in your word.
²⁵ They complained inside their tents,
    and did not listen to your voice, O LORD.

²⁶ So you raised your hand to them and swore
    that you would lay them low in the desert,
²⁷ would disperse their descendants through the
        nations
    and scatter them throughout the lands.

²⁸ They bowed before the Baal of Peor,
    ate offerings made to what is lifeless.
²⁹ They roused you to anger with their deeds,
    and a plague broke out among them.

³⁰ Then Phinehas stood up and intervened.
    Thus the plague was ended,
³¹ and this was counted to him as righteous
    from age to age forever.

³² They provoked you at the waters of Meribah.
 Through their fault it went ill with Moses,
³³ for they made his spirit grow bitter,
 and he uttered words that were rash.

³⁴ They failed to destroy the peoples,
 as you, O Lord, had commanded them;
³⁵ instead they mingled with the nations,
 and learned to act as they did.

³⁶ They also served their idols,
 and these became a snare to entrap them.
³⁷ They even offered their sons
 and their daughters in sacrifice to demons.

³⁸ They poured out innocent blood,
 the blood of their sons and daughters,
 whom they offered to the idols of Canaan.
 The land was polluted with blood.

³⁹ So they defiled themselves by their actions;
 their deeds were those of a harlot.
⁴⁰ Then your anger blazed against your people;
 you were filled with horror at your heritage.

⁴¹ So you handed them over to the nations,
 and their foes became their rulers.
⁴² Their enemies also oppressed them;
 they were subdued beneath their hand.

⁴³ Time after time you rescued them,
   but in their malice they dared to defy you,
   and were weakened even more by their guilt.
⁴⁴ In spite of this you paid heed to their distress,
   so often as you heard their cry.

⁴⁵ For their sake you remembered your covenant.
   In the greatness of your love, you relented,
⁴⁶ and let them be treated with compassion
   by all who held them captive.

⁴⁷ Save us, O Lord our God!
   And gather us from the nations,
   to give thanks to your holy name,
   and make it our glory to praise you.

                    *   *   *

[48] Blest be the Lord, God of Israel,
   forever, from age to age.
   Let all the people say,
   "Amen! Amen! Alleluia!"

BOOK FIVE
OF THE PSALTER

Psalm 107 (106)

¹ "O give thanks to the LORD who is good,
   whose faithful love endures forever."
² Let the redeemed of the LORD say this,
   those redeemed from the hand of the foe,
³ and gathered from far-off lands,
   from east and west, north and south.

⁴ They wandered in a barren desert,
   finding no way to a city they could dwell in.
⁵ Hungry they were and thirsty;
   their soul was fainting within them.

⁶ Then they cried to the LORD in their need,
   and God rescued them from their distress,
⁷ guiding them along a straight path,
   to reach a city they could dwell in.

⁸ Let them give thanks for the love of the LORD,
   such wonders for the human race:
⁹ God satisfies the thirsty soul,
   and fills the hungry with good things.

¹⁰ Some dwelt in darkness and the shadow of death,
   prisoners in misery and chains,
¹¹ having rebelled against the words of God,
   and spurned the plan of the Most High.
¹² God humbled their heart with toil.
   They stumbled; there was no one to help.

¹³ Then they cried to the LORD in their need,
   and God rescued them from their distress,
¹⁴ leading them out of darkness and the shadow of
        death,
   breaking their chains to pieces.

¹⁵ Let them give thanks for the love of the LORD,
   God's wonders for the human race:
¹⁶ God bursts the gates of bronze,
   and cuts through the iron bars.

¹⁷ Some fell sick on account of their sins,
   and were afflicted on account of their guilt.
¹⁸ They had a loathing for every food;
   they drew near to the gates of death.

¹⁹ Then they cried to the LORD in their need,
   and God rescued them from their distress,
²⁰ sending forth a word to heal them,
   saving their life from destruction.

21 Let them give thanks for the love of the LORD,
   God's wonders for the human race.
22 Let them offer a sacrifice of thanks,
   and tell of God's deeds with rejoicing.

23 Some went down to the sea in ships,
   to trade on the mighty waters.
24 These have seen the deeds of the LORD,
   the wonders done in the deep.

25 For the Lord spoke and raised up the storm-wind,
   tossing high the waves of the sea
26 that surged to heaven and dropped to the depths.
   Their souls melted away in their distress.

27 They staggered and reeled like drunkards,
   for all their skill was gone.
28 Then they cried to the LORD in their need,
   and God rescued them from their distress.

29 The Lord stilled the storm to a whisper,
   and the waves of the sea were hushed.
30 They rejoiced because of the calm,
   and God led them to the haven they desired.

31 Let them give thanks for the love of the LORD,
   God's wonders for the human race.
32 Let them exalt God in the people's assembly,
   praise the Lord in the meeting of the elders.

³³ The Lord changes rivers into desert,
   springs of water into thirsty ground,
³⁴ fruitful land into a salty waste,
   for the wickedness of those who live there.

³⁵ God changes desert into pools of water,
   thirsty ground into springs of water.
³⁶ There the hungry are settled,
   and they establish a city to dwell in.

³⁷ They sow fields and plant their vines,
   which yield an abundant harvest.
³⁸ God blesses them; they grow in numbers,
   God does not let their cattle decrease.

³⁹ They are diminished and brought low
   by oppression, evil, and sorrow.
⁴⁰ The Lord pours contempt upon princes,
   makes them wander in trackless wastes.

⁴¹ But God raises the needy from distress;
   makes families numerous as a flock.
⁴² The upright see it and rejoice,
   while all the wicked close their mouths.

⁴³ Whoever is wise should heed these things,
   and understand the loving mercy of the LORD.

Psalm 108 (107)

¹ *A Song. A Psalm of David.*

² My heart is ready, O God;
 my heart is ready.
 I will sing, I will sing your praise.
 Awake, my soul;
³ Awake, O lyre and harp.
 I will awake the dawn.

⁴ I will praise you, LORD, among the peoples;
 I will sing psalms to you among the nations,
⁵ for your faithful love is higher than the heavens,
 and your truth reaches the skies.

⁶ Be exalted, O God, above the heavens;
 may your glory shine on all the earth!
⁷ With your right hand, grant salvation and give
  answer;
 O come and deliver your friends.

⁸ From his holy place God has made this promise:
  "I will exult, and divide the land of Shechem;
  I will measure out the valley of Succoth.

⁹ Gilead is mine, as is Manasseh;
  Ephraim I take for my helmet,
  Judah is my scepter.
¹⁰ Moab is my washbowl;
  on Edom I will toss my shoe.
  Over Philistia I will shout in triumph."

¹¹ But who will lead me to the fortified city?
  Who will bring me to Edom?
¹² Have you not cast us off, O God?
  Will you march with our armies no longer?

¹³ Give us aid against the foe,
  for human help is vain.
¹⁴ With God, we shall do bravely;
  the Lord will trample down our foes.

Psalm 109 (108)

¹ *For the Choirmaster. Of David. A Psalm.*

O God whom I praise, do not be silent,
² for the mouths of deceit and wickedness
   are opened against me.

³ They speak to me with lying tongues;
   they beset me with words of hate,
   and attack me without cause.

⁴ In return for my love, they accuse me,
   while I am at prayer for them.
⁵ They repay me evil for good,
   hatred for love.

                    *   *   *

⁶ Appoint someone wicked as their judge;
   let an accuser stand at their right.
⁷ When judged, let them come out condemned;
   let their prayer be considered as sin.

⁸ Let the days of their lives be few;
   let another assume their office.
⁹ Let their children be fatherless orphans,
   and their wives become widows.

¹⁰ Let their children be wanderers and beggars,
    driven from the ruins of their home.
¹¹ Let the creditor seize all their goods;
    let strangers take the fruit of their work.

¹² Let no one show them any mercy,
nor pity their fatherless children.
¹³ Let their posterity be cut off,
in a generation their names blotted out.

¹⁴ Let their fathers' guilt be remembered to the LORD,
their mothers' sins be retained.
¹⁵ Let them always stand before the LORD,
that their memory be cut off from the earth.

¹⁶ For they did not think of showing mercy,
but pursued the poor and the needy,
hounding to death the brokenhearted.
¹⁷ They loved cursing; let curses fall on them.
They scorned blessing; let blessing pass them by.

¹⁸ They put on cursing like a coat:
let it sink into their bodies like water;
let it sink like oil into their bones.
¹⁹ Let it be like the clothes that cover them,
like belts they wear all the time.

²⁰ Let the LORD thus repay my accusers,
all those who speak evil against me.
²¹ But you, O LORD, my Lord,
do with me as befits your name.
How good your faithful love! Deliver me.

²² For I am poor and needy,
   and my heart is pierced within me.
²³ I fade like an evening shadow;
   I am shaken off like a locust.

²⁴ My knees are weak from fasting;
   my body is thin and gaunt.
²⁵ I have become an object of scorn;
   when they see me they shake their heads.

²⁶ Help me, LORD my God;
   save me with your faithful love.
²⁷ Let them know that this is your hand,
   that this is your doing, O LORD.

²⁸ They may curse, but you will bless.
   Let my attackers be put to shame,
   but let your servant rejoice.
²⁹ Let my accusers be clothed with dishonor,
   covered with shame as with a cloak.

³⁰ Loud thanks to the LORD are on my lips,
   with praise in the midst of the throng,
³¹ for the Lord stands at the right hand of the poor,
   to save their souls from those who condemn
      them.

Psalm 110 *(109)*

¹ *Of David. A Psalm.*

The LORD's revelation to my lord:
"Sit at my right hand,
until I make your foes your footstool."

² The LORD will send from Zion
your scepter of power:
rule in the midst of your foes.

³ With you is princely rule
on the day of your power.
In holy splendor, from the womb before the dawn,
I have begotten you.

⁴ The LORD has sworn an oath he will not change:
"You are a priest forever,
according to the order of Melchizedek."

⁵ The Lord at your right hand
shatters rulers on the day of God's wrath.

⁶ The Lord brings a judgment on the nations,
and heaps the bodies high,
and shatters heads throughout the wide earth.

⁷ He shall drink from the stream by the wayside,
and therefore he shall lift up his head.

Psalm 111 (110)

¹ Alleluia!

I will thank the LORD with all my heart,
in the meeting of the just and the assembly.
² Great are the works of the LORD,
to be pondered by all who delight in them.

³ Majestic and glorious your work;
your righteousness stands firm forever.
⁴ You have made a memorial of your wonders.
You, O LORD, are gracious and merciful.

⁵ You give food to those who revere you;
you are mindful of your covenant forever.
⁶ You have shown mighty works to your people
by giving them the heritage of nations.

⁷ Your handiwork is justice and truth,
your precepts are all of them sure,
⁸ standing firm forever and ever,
wrought in uprightness and truth.

⁹ You have sent redemption to your people,
and established your covenant forever.
Holy your name, to be feared.

¹⁰ Fear of the LORD is the beginning of wisdom;
understanding marks all who live by it.
Your praise endures forever!

Psalm 112 (111)

¹ Alleluia!

Blessed are those who fear the LORD,
who take great delight in God's commands.
² Their descendants shall be powerful on earth;
the generation of the upright will be blest.

³ Riches and wealth are in their houses;
their righteousness stands firm forever.
⁴ A light rises in the darkness for the upright;
they are generous, loving and righteous.

⁵ It goes well for those who deal generously and
lend,
who conduct their affairs with justice.
⁶ They will never be moved;
forever shall the righteous be remembered.

⁷ They have no fear of evil news;
with a firm heart, they trust in the LORD.
⁸ With steadfast hearts they will not fear;
they will see the downfall of their foes.

⁹ Openhanded, they give to the poor;
their righteousness stands firm forever.
Their might shall be exalted in glory.

¹⁰ The wicked see and are angry,
grind their teeth and fade away;
the desire of the wicked leads to doom.

Psalm 113 (112)

¹ Alleluia!

Praise, O servants of the LORD,
praise the name of the LORD!
² May the name of the LORD be blest
both now and forevermore!
³ From the rising of the sun to its setting,
praised be the name of the LORD!

⁴ High above all nations is the LORD,
above the heavens God's glory.
⁵ Who is like the LORD, our God,
who dwells on high,
⁶ who stoops from the heights to look down
upon heaven and earth?

⁷ From the dust the Lord lifts up the lowly,
from the ash heap raises the poor,
⁸ to set them in the company of leaders,
yes, with the leaders of the people.
⁹ To the childless wife God gives a home
as a joyful mother of children.

Psalm 114 (113A)

[1] Alleluia!

When Israel came forth from Egypt,
the house of Jacob from a foreign people,
[2] Judah became God's holy place,
Israel the Lord's domain.

[3] The sea beheld them and fled;
the Jordan turned back on its course.
[4] The mountains leapt like rams,
and the hills like yearling sheep.

[5] Why was it, sea, that you fled;
that you turned back, Jordan, on your course?
[6] O mountains, that you leapt like rams;
O hills, like yearling sheep?

[7] Tremble, O earth, before the Lord,
in the presence of the God of Jacob,
[8] who turns the rock into a pool,
and flint into a spring of water.

Psalm 115 *(113B)*

¹ Not to us, O LORD, not to us,
  but to your name give glory,
  for your faithful love and fidelity.
² Why should the nations say:
  "Where is their God?"

³ But our God is in the heavens,
  and wills whatever should be done.
⁴ Their idols are silver and gold,
  the work of human hands.

⁵ They have mouths but they cannot speak;
  they have eyes but they cannot see.
⁶ They have ears but they cannot hear;
  they have nostrils but they cannot smell.

⁷ They have hands but they cannot feel;
  they have feet but they cannot walk.
  They make no sound from their throats.
⁸ Their makers will come to be like them,
  as will all who trust in them.

⁹ House of Israel, trust in the LORD:
  their help and their shield is God.
¹⁰ House of Aaron, trust in the LORD:
  their help and their shield is God.
¹¹ You who fear the LORD, trust in the LORD:
  your help and your shield is God.

¹² The LORD remembers us and will bless us,
  will bless the house of Israel.
  God will bless the house of Aaron.

¹³ Those who fear the LORD will be blest,
  the little no less than the great.
¹⁴ To you may the LORD grant increase,
  to you and all your children.

¹⁵ May you be blest by the LORD,
  the maker of heaven and earth.
¹⁶ The heavens, the heavens belong to the LORD,
  but to the human race God has given the earth.

¹⁷ The dead shall not praise the LORD,
  nor those who go down into silence.
¹⁸ But we who live bless the LORD
  both now and forevermore.

  Alleluia!

Psalm 116A *(114:1–9; 115)*

¹ I love the Lᴏʀᴅ who has heard
   my voice, my appeal;
² For God has turned an ear to me
   whenever I call.

³ They surrounded me, the snares of death;
   the anguish of Sheol has found me;
   anguish and sorrow I found.
⁴ I called on the name of the Lᴏʀᴅ:
   "Deliver my soul, O Lᴏʀᴅ!"

⁵ How gracious is the Lᴏʀᴅ, and righteous;
   our God has compassion.
⁶ The Lᴏʀᴅ protects the simple;
   I was brought low, and was saved.

⁷ Turn back, my soul, to your rest,
   for the Lᴏʀᴅ has been good to you,
⁸ God has kept my soul from death,
   my eyes from tears, and my feet from stumbling.
⁹ I will walk in the presence of the Lᴏʀᴅ
   in the land of the living.

Psalm 116B (115:10–19)

10 I trusted, even when I said,
   "I am sorely afflicted,"
11 and when I said in my alarm,
   "All people are untruthful."

12 How can I repay the Lord
   for all the goodness shown to me?
13 The cup of salvation I will raise;
   I will call on the name of the Lord.

14 My vows to the Lord I will fulfill
   before all the people.
15 How precious in the eyes of the Lord
   is the death of God's faithful.

16 Your servant, Lord, your servant am I,
   you have loosened my bonds.
17 I will offer you a thanksgiving sacrifice;
   I will call on the name of the Lord.

18 My vows to the Lord I will fulfill
   before all the people,
19 in the courts of the house of the Lord,
   in your midst, O Jerusalem.

Alleluia!

Psalm 117 (116)

¹ O praise the LORD, all you nations;
acclaim God, all you peoples!

² For God's faithful love toward us is great;
the LORD remains faithful forever.

Alleluia!

Psalm 118 (117)

¹ Give thanks to the LORD, who is good,
   whose faithful love endures forever.

² Let the house of Israel say,
   "God's faithful love endures forever."
³ Let the house of Aaron say,
   "God's faithful love endures forever."
⁴ Let those who fear the LORD say,
   "God's faithful love endures forever."

⁵ I called to the LORD in my distress;
   the LORD has answered and freed me.
⁶ The LORD is at my side; I do not fear.
   What can anyone do against me?
⁷ The LORD is at my side as my helper;
   I shall look in triumph on my foes.

⁸ It is better to take refuge in the LORD
   than to trust in human beings;
⁹ it is better to take refuge in the LORD
   than to trust in rulers.

¹⁰ The nations all encircled me;
    in the name of the LORD I cut them off.
¹¹ They encircled me all around;
    in the name of the LORD I cut them off.

¹² They encircled me about like bees;
 they blazed like a fire among thorns.
 In the name of the LORD I cut them off.

¹³ They pushed me, pushed me hard to knock me
  down,
 but the LORD was my helper.
¹⁴ The LORD is my strength and my song,
 and has been my savior.

¹⁵ There are shouts of joy and salvation
 in the tents of the righteous.
 "The LORD's right hand has done mighty deeds;
¹⁶ The LORD's right hand is exalted.
 The LORD's right hand has done mighty deeds."

¹⁷ I shall not die, I shall live
 and recount the deeds of the LORD.
¹⁸ The LORD has punished me severely,
 but did not hand me over to death.

¹⁹ Open to me the gates of righteousness:
 I will enter and thank the LORD.
²⁰ This is the gate of the LORD,
 where the just may enter.
²¹ I will thank you, for you have answered,
 and you are my savior.

²² The stone that the builders rejected
  has become the cornerstone.
²³ By the LORD has this been done,
  a marvel in our eyes.
²⁴ This is the day the LORD has made;
  let us rejoice in it and be glad.

²⁵ We beseech you, O LORD, grant salvation;
  We beseech you, O LORD, grant success.
²⁶ Blest is he who comes
  in the name of the LORD.
  We bless you from the house of the LORD;
²⁷ the LORD is God, and has given us light.

  Go forward in procession with branches,
  as far as the horns of the altar.
²⁸ You are my God, I thank you.
  My God, I praise you.
²⁹ Give thanks to the LORD, who is good,
  whose faithful love endures forever.

Psalm 119 (118):1–8
Aleph

¹ Blessed are those whose way is blameless,
  who walk in the law of the Lord!
² Blessed are those who keep his decrees!
  With all their hearts they seek him.

³ They never do anything evil,
  but walk in God's ways.
⁴ You have laid down your precepts
  to be carefully kept.

⁵ May my ways be firm
  in keeping your statutes.
⁶ Then I shall not be put to shame
  as I fix my eyes on all your commands.

⁷ I will thank you with an upright heart,
  as I learn your righteous judgments.
⁸ I will keep your statutes;
  do not ever forsake me.

Psalm 119 (118):9–16
Beth

9 How shall a youth remain pure on life's way?
   By obeying your word.
10 I seek you with all my heart;
   let me not stray from your commands.

11 I treasure your word in my heart,
   lest I sin against you.
12 Blest are you, O LORD;
   teach me your statutes.

13 With my lips have I recounted
   all the decrees of your mouth.
14 I rejoice in the way of your precepts,
   as though all riches were mine.

15 I will ponder your precepts,
   and consider your paths.
16 I take delight in your statutes;
   I will not forget your word.

Psalm 119 (118):17–24
Gimel

[17] Deal bountifully with your servant,
   that I may live and keep your word.
[18] Open my eyes, that I may see
   the wonders of your law.

[19] I am a pilgrim in the land;
   hide not your commands from me.
[20] My soul is consumed with longing
   at all times for your decrees.

[21] You threaten the proud, the accursed,
   who stray from your commands.
[22] Free me from scorn and contempt,
   for I observe your decrees.

[23] Though princes sit plotting against me,
   your servant ponders your statutes.
[24] See, your decrees are my delight;
   your statutes are my counselors.

Psalm 119 (118):25–32
Daleth

²⁵ My soul holds fast to the dust;
   revive me by your word.
²⁶ I declared my ways and you answered me;
   teach me your statutes.

²⁷ Make me grasp the way of your precepts,
   and I will ponder your wonders.
²⁸ My soul pines away with grief;
   by your word raise me up.

²⁹ Keep me from the way of falsehood;
   grant me mercy by your law.
³⁰ I have chosen the way of faithfulness;
   your decrees I have upheld.

³¹ I cling to your decrees, O LORD;
   let me not be put to shame.
³² I will run the way of your commands;
   you open wide my heart.

Psalm 119 (118):*33–40*
He

³³ Lord, teach me the way of your statutes,
and I will keep them to the end.
³⁴ Grant me insight that I may keep your law,
and observe it wholeheartedly.

³⁵ Guide me in the path of your commands,
for in them is my delight.
³⁶ Bend my heart to your decrees,
and not to wrongful gain.

³⁷ Turn my eyes from gazing on vanities;
in your way, give me life.
³⁸ Fulfill your promise to your servant,
that you may be revered.

³⁹ Turn away the taunts I dread,
for your decrees are good.
⁴⁰ See, I long for your precepts;
give me life by your righteousness.

Psalm 119 (118):41–48
Vau

⁴¹ LORD, let your love come upon me,
    the salvation you have promised.
⁴² I shall answer those who taunt me,
    for I trust in your word.

⁴³ Never take the word of truth from my mouth,
    for I hope in your decrees.
⁴⁴ I shall always keep your law,
    forever and ever.

⁴⁵ I shall walk on a spacious plain,
    for I seek your precepts.
⁴⁶ I will speak of your decrees before rulers,
    and not be abashed.

⁴⁷ In your commands I have found my delight;
    these I have loved.
⁴⁸ I reach out to your commands, which I love,
    and ponder your statutes.

Psalm 119 (118):49–56
Zayin

⁴⁹ Remember your word to your servant,
   by which you made me hope.
⁵⁰ This is my comfort in sorrow:
   that your promise gives me life.

⁵¹ Though the proud may utterly deride me,
   I do not turn from your law.
⁵² When I remember your judgments of old,
   these, O Lord, console me.

⁵³ I am seized with indignation at the wicked
   who forsake your law.
⁵⁴ Your statutes have become my song
   wherever I dwell.

⁵⁵ I remember your name in the nighttime,
   and I keep your law.
⁵⁶ This has been my lot,
   for I have kept your precepts.

Psalm 119 (118):57–64
Heth

⁵⁷ You, O LORD, are my portion;
   I have promised to obey your words.
⁵⁸ With all my heart I implore your favor;
   as with your promise, have mercy.

⁵⁹ I have pondered my ways,
   and turned my steps to your decrees.
⁶⁰ I make haste; I do not delay
   to obey your commands.

⁶¹ Though the nets of the wicked ensnare me,
   your law I do not forget.
⁶² At midnight I will rise and thank you
   for your righteous decrees.

⁶³ I am a friend of all who revere you,
   who keep your precepts.
⁶⁴ O LORD, your faithful love fills the earth.
   Teach me your statutes.

Psalm 119 (118):65–72
Teth

[65] O LORD, you have been good to your servant,
according to your word.
[66] Teach me good judgment and knowledge,
for I trust in your commands.

[67] Before I was humbled, I strayed,
but now I keep your word.
[68] You are good, and you do what is good;
teach me your statutes.

[69] The arrogant smear me with lies;
with all my heart I keep your precepts.
[70] Their heart is dense like fat,
but your law is my delight.

[71] It was good for me to be humbled,
that I might learn your statutes.
[72] The law from your mouth means more to me
than large quantities of silver and gold.

Psalm 119 (118):73–80
Yod

⁷³ It was your hands that made me and shaped me;
   grant me insight to learn your commands.
⁷⁴ Those who revere you see me and rejoice,
   for I trust in your word.

⁷⁵ O Lord, I know that your decrees are right,
   and that in faithfulness, you humbled me.
⁷⁶ Let your faithful love console me
   by your promise to your servant.

⁷⁷ Show me compassion, that I may live,
   for your law is my delight.
⁷⁸ Let the arrogant be shamed who deflect me with
      lies;
   as for me, I will ponder your precepts.

⁷⁹ Let those who fear you turn to me,
   that they may know your decrees.
⁸⁰ Let my heart be blameless in your statutes,
   that I may not be put to shame.

Psalm 119 (118):81–88
Caph

81 My soul yearns for your salvation;
   I hope in your word.
82 My eyes yearn to see your promise.
   I ask, "When will you comfort me?"

83 I am like a wineskin shriveled by smoke,
   yet I remember your statutes.
84 How long must your servant endure?
   When will you bring judgment on my foes?

85 For me the proud have dug pitfalls;
   they defy your law.
86 Your commands are all true; then help me
   when lies oppress me.

87 They have almost made an end of me on earth,
   yet I forsake not your precepts.
88 In your faithful love, give me life;
   I will obey the decrees of your lips.

Psalm 119 (118):89–96
Lamed

89 Forever is your word, O LORD,
   standing firm in the heavens.
90 From age to age is your truth;
   like the earth, it stands firm.

91 Your judgments endure to this day,
   for all things are your servants.
92 Had your law not been my delight,
   I would have died in my affliction.

93 I will never forget your precepts,
   for with them you give me life.
94 Save me, I am yours,
   for I seek your precepts.

95 Though the wicked lie in wait to destroy me,
   yet I ponder your decrees.
96 I have seen that all perfection has an end,
   but your command is boundless.

Psalm 119 (118):97–104
Mem

97 O LORD, how I love your law:
    my meditation all the day!
98 Your command makes me wiser than my foes,
    for it is with me always.

99 I have more insight than all who teach me,
    for I ponder your decrees.
100 I have gained more understanding than my
        elders,
    for I keep your precepts.

101 I keep my feet from every evil path,
    to obey your word.
102 I have not turned away from your decrees;
    you yourself have taught me.

103 How sweet is your promise to my tongue,
    more than honey in the mouth.
104 I gain understanding from your precepts,
    and so I hate all false ways.

Psalm 119 (118):105–112
Nun

105 Your word is a lamp for my feet,
   and a light for my path.
106 I have sworn an oath and affirmed it,
   to obey your righteous judgments.

107 I am deeply afflicted, O LORD;
   by your word, give me life.
108 Accept, LORD, the homage of my lips,
   and teach me your decrees.

109 My life is in my hands at all times;
   I do not forget your law.
110 For me the wicked have set a snare;
   yet I do not stray from your precepts.

111 Your decrees are my heritage forever,
   the joy of my heart.
112 I incline my heart to carry out your statutes
   forever, to the end.

Psalm 119 (118):113–120
Samech

[113] I have hated doubtful thoughts,
   but I love your law.
[114] You are my hiding place, my shield;
   I hope in your word.

[115] Depart from me, you who do evil;
   I will keep my God's commands.
[116] Uphold me by your promise; I shall live.
   Let my hopes not be in vain.

[117] Bear me up and I shall be saved,
   and ever muse on your statutes.
[118] You spurn all who stray from your statutes;
   their cunning is in vain.

[119] You regard the wicked like dross,
   so I love your decrees.
[120] My flesh trembles in terror before you;
   I fear your judgments.

Psalm 119 (118):121–128
Ayin

¹²¹ I have done what is just and righteous;
   do not leave me to my foes.
¹²² Guarantee the well-being of your servant;
   let not the proud oppress me.

¹²³ My eyes grow weary as I watch for your
      salvation,
   and for your righteous promise.
¹²⁴ Treat your servant with your faithful love,
   and teach me your statutes.

¹²⁵ I am your servant; give me understanding:
   then I shall know your decrees.
¹²⁶ It is time for the LORD to act,
   for your law has been broken.

¹²⁷ That is why I love your commands
   more than finest gold,
¹²⁸ why I rule my life by your precepts,
   and hate false ways.

Psalm 119 (118):129–136
Pe

129 Your decrees are wonderful indeed;
   therefore my soul obeys them.
130 The unfolding of your word gives light,
   and understanding to the simple.

131 I have opened my mouth and I sigh,
   for I yearn for your commands.
132 Turn and have mercy on me,
   as is your rule for those who love your name.

133 Let my steps be guided by your promise;
   may evil never rule me.
134 Redeem me from human oppression,
   and I will keep your precepts.

135 Let your face shine forth on your servant,
   and teach me your decrees.
136 My eyes shed streams of tears,
   because of those who have not kept your law.

Psalm 119 (118):137–144
Tsade

[137] You are righteous, O LORD;
  your judgments are upright.
[138] You have imposed your decrees with righteousness,
  and with utter fidelity.

[139] I am consumed with zeal,
  for my foes forget your word.
[140] Your promise has been thoroughly tested,
  and it is cherished by your servant.

[141] Although I am young and despised,
  I do not forget your precepts.
[142] Your righteousness is righteous forever,
  and your law is truth.

[143] Though anguish and distress have found me,
  your commands are my delight.
[144] Your decrees are forever just;
  give me insight, and I shall live.

Psalm 119 (118):145–152
Koph

¹⁴⁵ I call with all my heart; LORD, answer me.
I will observe your statutes.
¹⁴⁶ I call upon you; save me,
and I will keep your decrees.

¹⁴⁷ I rise before dawn and cry for help;
I have hoped in your word.
¹⁴⁸ My eyes awaken before dawn,
to ponder your promise.

¹⁴⁹ In your mercy, hear my voice, O LORD;
give me life by your decrees.
¹⁵⁰ Those who pursue me with malice draw near;
they are far from your law.

¹⁵¹ But you, O LORD, are close;
all your commands are truth.
¹⁵² From of old I have known that your decrees
are established forever.

Psalm 119 (118):153–160
Resh

¹⁵³ See my affliction and deliver me,
for I do not forget your law.
¹⁵⁴ Uphold my cause and redeem me;
by your promise, give me life.

¹⁵⁵ Salvation is far from the wicked,
who are heedless of your statutes.
¹⁵⁶ Numberless, LORD, are your mercies;
in your justice, give me life.

¹⁵⁷ Though my foes and oppressors are countless,
I have not swerved from your decrees.
¹⁵⁸ I look at the faithless with disgust;
they have not kept your word.

¹⁵⁹ See how I love your precepts, O LORD!
In your mercy, give me life.
¹⁶⁰ Truth is the sum of your word;
all your righteous judgments are eternal.

Psalm 119 (118):161–168
Shin

¹⁶¹ Though princes oppress me without cause,
 my heart reveres your word.
¹⁶² I rejoice at your promise,
 like one who finds a great treasure.

¹⁶³ Falsehood I hate and detest,
 but I love your law.
¹⁶⁴ Seven times a day I praise you
 for your righteous decrees.

¹⁶⁵ The lovers of your law have great peace;
 no stumbling block for them.
¹⁶⁶ I await your salvation, O Lord;
 I fulfill your commands.

¹⁶⁷ My soul obeys your decrees,
 and loves them dearly.
¹⁶⁸ I obey your precepts and decrees;
 all my ways are before you.

Psalm 119 (118):169–176
Tau

169 Let my cry come before you, O LORD;
  give me insight by your word.
170 Let my pleading come before you;
  rescue me according to your promise.

171 My lips shall proclaim your praise,
  because you teach me your statutes.
172 My tongue will sing of your promise,
  for your commands are righteous.

173 Let your hand be ready to help me,
  for I have chosen your precepts.
174 I long for your salvation, O LORD,
  and your law is my delight.

175 My soul shall live and praise you.
  Your judgments give me help.
176 I have strayed like a sheep; seek your servant;
  for I do not forget your commands.

Psalm 120 (119)

¹ *A Song of Ascents.*

To the LORD in the hour of my distress
I call—and am answered.
² "O LORD, save my soul from lying lips,
from the tongue of the deceitful."

³ What should God give you, what repay you,
O deceitful tongue?
⁴ The warrior's arrows sharpened,
with red-hot coals from the broom tree!

⁵ Alas, that I sojourn in Meshech,
dwell among the tents of Kedar!
⁶ I have had enough of dwelling
with those who hate peace.
⁷ I am for peace, but when I speak,
they are for war.

Psalm 121 (120)

¹ *A Song of Ascents.*

I lift up my eyes to the mountains;
from where shall come my help?
² My help shall come from the Lord,
who made heaven and earth.

³ The Lord will keep your foot from stumbling.
Your guard will never slumber.
⁴ No, the guardian of Israel
neither sleeps nor slumbers.

⁵ The Lord your guard, the Lord your shade
at your right hand.
⁶ By day the sun shall not smite you,
nor the moon in the night.

⁷ The Lord will guard you from evil,
will guard your soul.
⁸ The Lord will guard your going and coming,
both now and forever.

Psalm 122 (121)

¹ *A Song of Ascents. Of David.*

I rejoiced when they said to me,
"Let us go to the house of the LORD."
² And now our feet are standing
within your gates, O Jerusalem.

³ Jerusalem is built as a city
bonded as one together.
⁴ It is there that the tribes go up,
the tribes of the LORD,
as is decreed for Israel
to give thanks to the name of the LORD.

⁵ There were set the thrones for judgment,
the thrones of the house of David.
⁶ For the peace of Jerusalem pray,
"May they prosper, those who love you."
⁷ May peace abide in your walls,
and security be in your towers.

⁸ For the sake of my family and friends,
let me say, "Peace upon you."
⁹ For the sake of the house of the LORD, our God,
I will seek good things for you.

Psalm 123 *(122)*

¹ *A Song of Ascents.*

To you have I lifted up my eyes,
you who dwell in the heavens.

² Behold, like the eyes of slaves
on the hand of their lords,
like the eyes of a servant
on the hand of her mistress,
so our eyes are on the LORD our God,
till mercy be shown us.

³ Have mercy on us, LORD, have mercy.
We are filled with contempt.
⁴ Indeed, all too full is our soul
with the scorn of the arrogant,
the disdain of the proud.

Psalm 124 (123)

¹ *A Song of Ascents. Of David.*

"If the LORD had not been on our side,"
let Israel say –
² "If the LORD had not been on our side
when people rose against us,
³ then would they have swallowed us alive
when their anger was kindled.

⁴ "Then would the waters have engulfed us,
the torrent gone over us;
⁵ over our head would have swept
the raging waters."

⁶ Blest be the LORD who did not give us
as prey to their teeth!
⁷ Our life, like a bird, has escaped
from the snare of the fowler.

Indeed, the snare has been broken,
and we have escaped.
⁸ Our help is in the name of the LORD,
who made heaven and earth.

Psalm 125 *(124)*

¹ *A Song of Ascents.*

Those who put their trust in the LORD
are like Mount Zion, that cannot be shaken,
that stands forever.
² Jerusalem! The mountains surround her;
so the LORD surrounds this people,
both now and forever.

³ For the scepter of the wicked shall not rest
over the land of the righteous,
for fear that the hands of the righteous
should turn to evil.

⁴ Do good, LORD, to those who are good,
to the upright of heart;
⁵ but those who turn to crooked ways
the LORD will drive away with the wicked!
On Israel, peace!

Psalm 126 (125)

¹ *A Song of Ascents.*

When the LORD brought back the exiles of Zion,
we thought we were dreaming.
² Then was our mouth filled with laughter;
on our tongues, songs of joy.

Then they said among the nations,
"What great deeds the LORD worked for them!"
³ What great deeds the LORD worked for us!
Indeed, we were glad.

⁴ Bring back our exiles, O LORD,
as streams in the Negeb.
⁵ Those who are sowing in tears
will sing when they reap.

⁶ They go out, they go out, full of tears,
bearing seed for the sowing;
they come back, they come back with a song,
bearing their sheaves.

Psalm 127 (126)

[1] *A Song of Ascents. Of Solomon.*

If the LORD does not build the house,
in vain do its builders labor;
if the LORD does not guard the city,
in vain does the guard keep watch.

[2] In vain is your earlier rising,
your going later to rest,
you who toil for the bread you eat,
when God pours gifts on his beloved while they
slumber.

[3] Yes, children are a gift from the LORD,
a reward, the fruit of the womb.
[4] Like arrows in the hand of a warrior,
so are the children of one's youth.

[5] Blessed are the warriors
who have filled their quivers with these arrows!
They will have no cause for shame,
when they dispute with their foes in the gateways.

Psalm 128 *(127)*

¹ *A Song of Ascents.*

Blessed are all who fear the Lord,
and walk in God's ways!
² By the labor of your hands you shall eat.
You will be blessed and prosper.

³ Your wife is like a fruitful vine
in the heart of your house;
your children like shoots of the olive
around your table.
⁴ Indeed thus shall be blessed
the husband who fears the Lord.

⁵ May the Lord bless you from Zion.
May you see Jerusalem prosper
all the days of your life!
⁶ May you see your children's children.
On Israel, peace!

Psalm 129 *(128)*

¹ *A Song of Ascents.*

"They have pressed me hard from my youth,"
   let Israel sing.
² "They have pressed me hard from my youth,
   but could never overcome me.

³ The plowers plowed my back,
   drawing long furrows.
⁴ Yet the LORD, who is righteous,
   has cut the cords of the wicked."

⁵ Let them be shamed and routed,
   all those who hate Zion!
⁶ Let them be like grass on the roof
   that withers before it flowers.

⁷ With that no reapers fill their hands,
   no binders of sheaves their arms.
⁸ And those passing by will not say,
   "The blessing of the LORD be upon you!"
   We bless you in the name of the LORD!

Psalm 130 (129)

Out of the depths I cry to you, O LORD;
² Lord, hear my voice!
O let your ears be attentive
to the sound of my pleadings.

³ If you, O LORD, should mark iniquities,
Lord, who could stand?
⁴ But with you is found forgiveness,
that you may be revered.

⁵ I wait for the LORD, my soul waits.
I hope in God's word.
⁶ My soul is waiting for the Lord,
more than sentinels for daybreak.

More than sentinels for daybreak,
⁷ let Israel wait for the LORD.
For with the LORD there is loving mercy,
in God is plentiful redemption.
⁸ It is the Lord who will redeem Israel
from all its iniquities.

Psalm 131 *(130)*

¹ *A Song of Ascents. Of David.*

O LORD, my heart is not proud,
nor haughty my eyes.
I have not gone after things too great,
nor marvels beyond me.

² Truly, I have set my soul
in tranquility and silence.
As a weaned child on its mother,
as a weaned child is my soul within me.

³ O Israel, hope in the LORD,
both now and forever.

Psalm 132 *(131)*

¹ *A Song of Ascents.*

O LORD, remember David
and all the hardships he endured,
² the oath he swore to the LORD,
his vow to the Strong One of Jacob.

³ "I will not enter the house where I dwell,
nor go to the bed where I rest;
⁴ I will give no sleep to my eyes,
to my eyelids I will give no slumber,
⁵ till I find a place for the LORD,
a dwelling for the Strong One of Jacob."

⁶ We heard of it at Ephrata;
we found it in the plains of Yearim.
⁷ "Let us go to the place of God's dwelling;
let us bow down at God's footstool."

⁸ Go up, LORD, to the place of your rest,
you and the ark of your strength.
⁹ Your priests shall be clothed with righteousness;
your faithful shall ring out their joy.
¹⁰ For the sake of David your servant,
do not reject your anointed.

¹¹ The LORD swore an oath to David;
God will not go back on his word:
"A son, the fruit of your body,
will I set upon your throne.

¹² If your sons hold fast to my covenant,
and my decrees that I shall teach them,
their sons, in turn, shall sit
on your throne from age to age."

¹³ For the LORD has chosen Zion,
has desired it for a dwelling:
¹⁴ "This is my resting place from age to age;
here have I desired to dwell.

¹⁵ "I will greatly bless her produce;
I will fill her poor with bread.
¹⁶ I will clothe her priests with salvation,
and her faithful shall ring out their joy.

¹⁷ "I will make a stock sprout up for David;
I will prepare a lamp for my anointed.
¹⁸ I will cover his enemies with shame,
but on him my crown shall shine."

Psalm 133 (132)

¹ *A Song of Ascents. Of David.*

How good and how pleasant it is,
when a family lives in unity!

² It is like precious oil upon the head
running down upon the beard,
running down upon Aaron's beard,
upon the collar of his robes;

³ Like the dew of Hermon, which runs down
on the mountains of Zion.
For there the LORD bestows a blessing:
life forever.

Psalm 134 *(133)*

¹ A Song of Ascents.

O come and bless the LORD,
all you servants of the LORD,
who stand by night in the house of the LORD.
² Lift up your hands to the holy place,
and bless the LORD.

³ May the LORD bless you from Zion,
who made both heaven and earth.

Psalm 135 (134)

1 Alleluia!

Praise the name of the LORD;
give praise, O servants of the LORD,
2 who stand in the house of the LORD,
in the courts of the house of our God.

3 Praise the LORD, for the LORD is good.
Sing a psalm to God's name, who is gracious.
4 For the LORD has chosen Jacob,
and Israel as a treasured possession.

5 For I know that the LORD is great,
that our Lord is high above all gods.
6 Whatever the LORD wills is accomplished,
in heaven, and on earth,
in the seas, and in all the depths.

7 God summons clouds from the ends of the earth,
makes lightning produce the rain,
sends forth the wind from heaven's treasuries.

8 The Lord smote the firstborn of the Egyptians,
human beings and beasts alike.
9 God sent signs and wonders in your midst, O
Egypt,
against Pharaoh and all his servants.
10 Nations in great numbers were struck,
and kings in their might were subdued:

¹¹ Sihon, king of the Amorites,
   Og, the king of Bashan,
   and all the kingdoms of Canaan.
¹² God gave their land as a heritage,
   a heritage to Israel, God's people.

¹³ LORD, your name stands forever,
   your renown, LORD, from age to age.
¹⁴ For the LORD will vindicate this people
   and take pity on God's servants.

¹⁵ Pagan idols are silver and gold,
   the work of human hands.
¹⁶ They have mouths but they do not speak;
   they have eyes but they do not see.

¹⁷ They have ears but they do not hear;
   there is never a breath on their lips.
¹⁸ Their makers will come to be like them,
   and so will all who trust in them!

¹⁹ House of Israel, bless the LORD!
   House of Aaron, bless the LORD!
²⁰ House of Levi, bless the LORD!
   You who fear the LORD, bless the LORD!
²¹ From Zion may the LORD be blest,
   God, who dwells in Jerusalem!

   Alleluia!

Psalm 136 (135)

¹ O give thanks to the LORD, who is good,
  for God's faithful love endures forever.
² Give thanks to the God of gods,
  for God's faithful love endures forever.
³ Give thanks to the Lord of lords,
  for God's faithful love endures forever.

⁴ Who alone has wrought marvelous works,
  for God's faithful love endures forever.
⁵ who in wisdom made the heavens,
  for God's faithful love endures forever;
⁶ who spread the earth on the waters,
  for God's faithful love endures forever.

⁷ It was the Lord who made the great lights,
  for God's faithful love endures forever;
⁸ the sun to rule in the day,
  for God's faithful love endures forever;
⁹ the moon and the stars in the night,
  for God's faithful love endures forever.

¹⁰ The firstborn of the Egyptians the Lord smote,
  for God's faithful love endures forever;
¹¹ brought Israel out from their midst,
  for God's faithful love endures forever;
¹² with mighty hand and outstretched arm,
  for God's faithful love endures forever.

¹³ The Lord divided the Red Sea in two,
    for God's faithful love endures forever;
¹⁴ made Israel pass through the midst,
    for God's faithful love endures forever;
¹⁵ flung Pharaoh and his force in the Red Sea,
    for God's faithful love endures forever.

¹⁶ The Lord led the people through the desert,
    for God's faithful love endures forever.
¹⁷ Kings in their greatness he struck down,
    for God's faithful love endures forever.
¹⁸ Kings in their splendor the Lord slew,
    for God's faithful love endures forever.

¹⁹ Sihon, king of the Amorites,
    for God's faithful love endures forever;
²⁰ and Og, the king of Bashan,
    for God's faithful love endures forever.

²¹ The Lord gave their land as a heritage,
    for God's faithful love endures forever;
²² A heritage for Israel, God's servant,
    for God's faithful love endures forever.
²³ The Lord remembered us in our distress,
    for God's faithful love endures forever.

²⁴ The Lord snatched us away from our foes,
    for God's faithful love endures forever.
²⁵ The Lord gives bread to all mortal flesh,
    for God's faithful love endures forever.
²⁶ To the God of heaven give thanks,
    for God's faithful love endures forever.

Psalm 137 (136)

¹ By the rivers of Babylon
 there we sat and wept,
 remembering Zion;
² on the poplars that grew there
 we hung up our harps.

³ For it was there that they asked us,
 our captors, for songs,
 our oppressors, for joy.
 "Sing to us," they said,
 "one of Zion's songs."

⁴ O how could we sing
 the song of the LORD
 on foreign soil?
⁵ If I forget you, Jerusalem,
 let my right hand wither!

⁶ O let my tongue hold fast to my palate
 if I remember you not,
 if I prize not Jerusalem, the first of my joys!

⁷ Remember, O Lᴏʀᴅ,
  against the children of Edom
  the day of Jerusalem,
  when they said, "Tear it down!
  Tear it down to its foundations!"

⁸ O daughter Babylon, destroyer,
  blessed who repays you the payment you paid to
      us!
⁹ Blessed who grasps and shatters your children on
      the rock!

Psalm 138 (137)

¹ *Of David.*

I thank you, Lᴏʀᴅ, with all my heart;
you have heard the words of my mouth.
In the presence of the angels I praise you.
² I bow down toward your holy temple.

I give thanks to your name
for you have exalted over all
your name and your promise.
³ On the day I called, you answered me;
you increased the strength of my soul.

⁴ All earthly rulers shall thank you, O Lᴏʀᴅ,
when they hear the words of your mouth.
⁵ They shall sing of the ways of the Lᴏʀᴅ,
"How great is the glory of the Lᴏʀᴅ!"

⁶ The Lᴏʀᴅ is high, yet looks on the lowly,
and the haughty God knows from afar.
⁷ You give me life though I walk amid affliction;
you stretch out your hand against the anger of my
        foes.

With your right hand you save me;
⁸ the Lᴏʀᴅ will accomplish this for me.
O Lᴏʀᴅ, your merciful love is eternal;
discard not the work of your hands.

Psalm 139 (138)

¹ *For the Choirmaster. Of David. A Psalm.*

O LORD, you search me and you know me.
² You yourself know my resting and my rising;
  you discern my thoughts from afar.
³ You mark when I walk or lie down;
  you know all my ways through and through.

⁴ Before ever a word is on my tongue,
  you know it, O LORD, through and through.
⁵ Behind and before, you besiege me,
  your hand ever laid upon me.
⁶ Too wonderful for me, this knowledge;
  too high, beyond my reach.

⁷ O where can I go from your spirit,
  or where can I flee from your face?
⁸ If I climb the heavens, you are there.
  If I lie in Sheol, you are there.

⁹ If I take the wings of the dawn
  or dwell at the sea's furthest end,
¹⁰ even there your hand would lead me;
  your right hand would hold me fast.

¹¹ If I say, "Let the darkness hide me
and the light around me be night,"
¹² even darkness is not dark to you,
but night will be bright as the day,
and darkness the same as the light.

¹³ For it was you who formed my inmost being,
knit me together in my mother's womb.
¹⁴ I thank you who wonderfully made me;
how wonderful are your works,
which my soul knows well!

¹⁵ My frame was not hidden from you,
when I was being fashioned in secret
and molded in the depths of the earth.

¹⁶ Your eyes saw me yet unformed;
and all days are recorded in your book,
formed before one of them came into being.

¹⁷ To me how precious your thoughts, O God;
how great is the sum of them!
¹⁸ If I count them, they are more than the sand;
at the end I am still at your side.

¹⁹ O God, that you would slay the wicked;
   let the bloodthirsty depart from me!
²⁰ With deceit they speak against you,
   and against you, they exalt themselves in vain.

²¹ Do I not hate those who hate you,
   abhor those who rise against you?
²² I hate them with a perfect hate,
   and they are foes to me.

²³ O search me, God, and know my heart.
   O test me, and know my thoughts.
²⁴ See that my path is not wicked,
   and lead me in the way everlasting.

Psalm 140 *(139)*

¹ *For the Choirmaster. A Psalm of David.*

² Rescue me, LORD, from the wicked;
  from the violent keep me safe,
³ from those who plan evil in their hearts,
  and stir up strife every day,
⁴ who sharpen their tongue like an adder's,
  with the poison of viper on their lips.

⁵ LORD, guard me from the hands of the wicked;
  from the violent keep me safe;
  they plan to make me stumble.
⁶ The proud have hidden a trap,
  have spread out lines in a net,
  set snares across my path.

⁷ I have said to the LORD, "You are my God."
  Give ear, O LORD, to the cry of my appeal!
⁸ LORD, my Lord, my mighty help,
  you shield my head in the battle.
⁹ Do not grant, O LORD, the wicked their desire,
  nor let their plots succeed.

¹⁰ Those surrounding me lift up their heads.
  Let the malice of their speech overwhelm them.
¹¹ Let coals of fire rain upon them.
  Let them be flung in the abyss, no more to rise.
¹² Let no slanderer stand firm upon the earth.
  Let evil trap the violent to their ruin!

¹³ I know the Lord will avenge the poor,
  that God will do justice for the needy.
¹⁴ Truly the righteous will give thanks to your
      name;
  the upright shall live in your presence.

Psalm 141 (140)

¹ *A Psalm of David.*

I have called to you, LORD; O hasten to help me!
Hear my voice when I cry to you.
² Let my prayer be as incense before you,
the raising of my hands like an evening oblation.

³ Set, O LORD, a guard on my mouth;
keep watch at the door of my lips!
⁴ Do not turn my heart to things that are evil,
to wicked deeds with those who are sinners.

Never allow me to share in their feasting.
⁵ If someone righteous strikes me it is kindness;
but let the oil of the wicked not anoint my head.
Let my prayer be ever against their malice.

⁶ If they fall into the merciless hands of their judges,
they will grasp how kind are my words.
⁷ As clods of earth plowed up on the ground,
so their bones were strewn at the mouth of Sheol.

⁸ To you my eyes are turned, O LORD, my Lord.
In you I take refuge; spare my soul!
⁹ From the trap they have laid for me, keep me safe;
keep me from the snares of those who do evil.

¹⁰Let the wicked together fall into their traps,
while I pursue my way unharmed.

Psalm 142 (141)

¹ *A Maskil of David when he was in the cave.*
   A Prayer.

² With my voice I cry to you, O Lord;
   with my voice I entreat you, O Lord.
³ I pour out my trouble before you;
   I recount to you all my distress
⁴ while my spirit faints within me.
   But you, O Lord, know my path.

   On the way where I shall walk,
   they have hidden a snare to entrap me.
⁵ Look on my right hand and see:
   there is no one who pays me heed.
   No escape remains open to me;
   no one cares for my soul.

⁶ To you I cry, O Lord.
   I have said, "You are my refuge,
   my portion in the land of the living."
⁷ Listen, then, to my cry,
   for I am brought down very low.

   Rescue me from those who pursue me,
   for they are stronger than I.
⁸ Bring my soul out of prison,
   and I shall give thanks to your name.
   Around me the righteous will assemble,
   because of your goodness to me.

Psalm 143 (142)

¹ *A Psalm of David.*

Listen, O LORD, to my prayer;
turn your ear to my appeal.
You are faithful, you are righteous; give answer.
² Do not call your servant to judgment,
for in your sight no living being is righteous.

³ The foe has pursued my soul,
has crushed my life to the ground,
and has made me dwell in darkness,
like those long dead.
⁴ Therefore my spirit fails;
my heart is desolate within me.

⁵ I remember the days that are past;
I ponder all your works.
I muse on what your hand has wrought,
⁶ and to you I stretch out my hands.
My soul is like a parched land before you.

⁷ O LORD, make haste and answer me,
  for my spirit fails within me.
  Do not hide your face from me,
  lest I become like those going down to the pit.

⁸ In the morning, let me hear your faithful love,
  for in you I place my trust.
  Make me know the way I should walk;
  to you I lift up my soul.

⁹ Rescuc me, O LORD, from my foes;
  to you have I fled for refuge.
¹⁰ Teach me to do your will,
  for you are my God.
  Let your good spirit guide me
  upon ground that is level.

¹¹ LORD, save my life for the sake of your name;
  in your righteousness, lead my soul out of
        distress.
¹² In your mercy make an end of my foes;
  destroy all those who oppress my soul,
  for I am your servant.

Psalm 144 *(143)*

¹ *Of David.*

Blest be the LORD, my rock,
who trains my hands for battle,
my fingers for war.

² God is my love, my fortress,
my stronghold, my savior,
my shield in whom I take refuge,
who subdues the peoples under me.

³ LORD, who are we that you regard us so,
mere human beings, that you keep us in mind,
⁴ people who are merely a breath,
whose days are like a passing shadow?

⁵ Lower your heavens, O LORD, and come down.
Touch the mountains; wreathe them in smoke.
⁶ Flash your lightnings; rout the foe.
Shoot your arrows, and put them to flight.

⁷ Reach down with your hand from on high;
rescue me, save me from the many waters,
from the hands of foreign foes
⁸ whose mouths speak empty words,
whose hands are raised in perjury.

⁹ To you, O God, will I sing a new song;
   I will play on the ten-stringed harp
¹⁰ to you who give kings their victory,
   who redeemed your servant David,
   from the evil sword.

¹¹ Rescue me, free me from the hands of foreign
        foes,
   whose mouths speak lies,
   whose right hands are raised in perjury.

¹² Let our sons then flourish like saplings,
   grown tall and strong from their youth;
   our daughters graceful as columns,
   as though they were carved for a palace.

¹³ Let our barns be filled to overflowing
   with crops of every kind;
   our sheep increasing by thousands,
   tens of thousands in our fields,
¹⁴ our cattle heavy with young.

   No ruined wall, no exile,
   no sound of weeping in our streets.
¹⁵ Blessed the people of whom this is true;
   blessed the people whose God is the LORD!

Psalm 145 (144)

¹ *Praise. Of David.*

I will extol you, my God and King,
and bless your name forever and ever.

² I will bless you day after day,
and praise your name forever and ever.
³ The LORD is great and highly to be praised;
God's greatness cannot be measured.

⁴ Age to age shall proclaim your works,
shall declare your mighty deeds.
⁵ They will tell of your great glory and splendor,
and recount your wonderful works.

⁶ They will speak of your awesome deeds,
recount your greatness and might.
⁷ They will recall your abundant goodness,
and sing of your righteous deeds with joy.

⁸ The LORD is kind and full of compassion,
slow to anger, abounding in mercy.
⁹ How good are you, O LORD, to all,
compassionate to all your creatures.

¹⁰ All your works shall thank you, O LORD,
and all your faithful ones bless you.
¹¹ They shall speak of the glory of your reign,
and declare your mighty deeds,

¹² To make known your might to the whole human
race,
and the glorious splendor of your reign.
¹³ Your kingdom is an everlasting kingdom;
your rule endures for all generations.

You are faithful, LORD, in all your words,
and holy in all your deeds.
¹⁴ You, LORD, support all who fall,
and raise up all who are bowed down.

¹⁵ The eyes of all look to you,
and you give them their food in due season.
¹⁶ You open your hand and satisfy
the desire of every living thing.

¹⁷ You are righteous, O LORD, in all your ways,
and holy in all your deeds.
¹⁸ You are close, LORD, to all who call on you,
who call on you in truth.

¹⁹ You fulfill the desires of those who fear you;
you hear their cry and save them.
²⁰ You keep watch, LORD, over all who love you;
but the wicked you will utterly destroy.

²¹ Let my mouth speak the praise of the LORD;
let all flesh bless the holy name
forever, for ages unending.

Psalm 146 *(145)*

¹ Alleluia!

My soul, give praise to the LORD;
² I will praise the LORD all my life,
  sing praise to my God while I live.

³ Put no trust in rulers,
  in human beings who cannot save.
⁴ Take their breath, they return to the earth,
  and their plans that day come to nothing.

⁵ Blessed the one who is helped by Jacob's God,
  whose hope is in the LORD our God,
⁶ who made the heavens and the earth,
  the seas and all they contain,

Who preserves fidelity forever,
⁷ who does justice to those who are oppressed.
  who furnishes bread to the hungry;
  the LORD who sets prisoners free,
⁸ the LORD who opens the eyes of the blind,
  the LORD who raises up those who are bowed
    down.

It is the LORD who loves the righteous,
9 the LORD who protects the stranger
and upholds the orphan and the widow,
but thwarts the path of the wicked.
10 The LORD will reign forever,
your God, O Zion, from age to age.

Alleluia!

Psalm 147A (146:1–11)

Alleluia!

1 How good to sing psalms to our God;
   how pleasant to chant fitting praise!

2 The LORD builds up Jerusalem
   and brings back Israel's exiles;
3 God heals the brokenhearted,
   and binds up all their wounds;
4 God counts out the number of the stars,
   and calls each one by its name.

5 Our Lord is great and almighty;
   God's wisdom can never be measured.
6 The LORD lifts up the lowly,
   and casts down the wicked to the ground.
7 O sing to the LORD, giving thanks;
   sing psalms to our God with the lyre.

8 The Lord covers the heavens with clouds;
   and prepares the rain for the earth,
   making mountains sprout with grass,
   and plants to serve human needs.

9 God provides the cattle with their food,
   and what young ravens call for.
10 The Lord's delight is not in the strength of horses,
    nor God's pleasure in a warrior's stride.
11 The LORD delights in those who revere him,
    those who wait for God's faithful love.

Psalm 147B *(147)*

¹² O Jerusalem, glorify the Lord!
    O Zion, praise your God,
¹³ who has strengthened the bars of your gates,
    and has blessed your children within you;
¹⁴ who established peace on your borders,
    and gives you your fill of finest wheat.

¹⁵ The Lord sends out his word to the earth;
    the divine command runs swiftly.
¹⁶ God showers down snow like wool,
    and scatters hoarfrost like ashes.

¹⁷ The Lord hurls down hailstones like crumbs;
    before such cold, who can stand?
¹⁸ God sends forth a word and it melts them;
    at the blowing of God's breath the waters flow.

¹⁹ The Lord reveals a word to Jacob;
    to Israel, decrees and judgments.
²⁰ God has not dealt thus with other nations,
    has not taught them heaven's judgments.

Alleluia!

Psalm 148

¹ Alleluia!

Praise the LORD from the heavens;
  praise the Lord in the heights.
² Praise the Lord, all his angels;
  praise the Lord, all his hosts.

³ Praise the Lord, sun and moon;
  praise the Lord, all shining stars.
⁴ Praise the Lord, highest heavens,
  and the waters above the heavens.

⁵ Let them praise the name of the LORD,
  who commanded, and they were created.
⁶ God established them forever and ever,
  gave a law which shall not pass away.

⁷ Praise the LORD from the earth,
  sea creatures and all ocean depths,
⁸ fire and hail, snow and mist,
  stormy winds that fulfill the command;

⁹ Mountains and all hills,
  fruit trees and all cedars,
¹⁰ beasts, both wild and tame,
  creeping things and birds on the wing;

¹¹ Rulers of the earth and all peoples,
  sovereigns and all judges of the earth,
¹² young men and maidens as well,
  the old and the young together.

¹³ Let them praise the name of the LORD,
  for God's name alone is exalted,
  whose splendor rises above heaven and earth.

¹⁴ The Lord exalts the strength of the people,
  and is the praise of all the faithful,
  the praise of the children of Israel,
  of the people to whom our God is close.

Alleluia!

Psalm 149

¹ Alleluia!

Sing a new song to the LORD,
high praise in the assembly of the faithful.
² Let Israel rejoice in its Maker;
let Zion's children exult in their King.
³ Let them praise God's name with dancing,
and make music with timbrel and lyre.

⁴ For the LORD takes delight in the people,
and adorns the poor with salvation.
⁵ Let the faithful rejoice in glory,
shout with joy on their couches.
⁶ Let the praise of God be in their mouths
and a two-edged sword in their hands,

⁷ To deal out vengeance to the nations
and punishment upon the peoples;
⁸ to bind their rulers in chains
and their nobles in fetters of iron;
⁹ to carry out the judgment decreed.
This is an honor for all God's faithful.

Alleluia!

Psalm 150

¹ Alleluia!

Praise God in the holy temple;
  praise the Lord in the mighty firmament.
² Praise God for powerful deeds;
  for boundless grandeur, praise God.

³ O praise the Lord with sound of trumpet;
  give praise with lute and harp.
⁴ Praise God with timbrel and dance;
  give praise with strings and pipes.

⁵ O praise God with resounding cymbals;
  give praise with clashing of cymbals.
⁶ Let everything that breathes praise the LORD!

Alleluia!